By R. Eric Thomas

Here for It

Kings of B'more

Congratulations, The Best Is Over!

Contents

Introduction: The Middle

I wanted a cupcake. I was in my late twenties and, all my other ambitions thwarted, I just wanted a cupcake. But you can't make one cupcake. So I made a dozen cupcakes. Why not? I deserved a little treat!

It takes effort, but it's not the hardest conceivable dessert. I wasn't treating myself to a croquembouche. I'm the kind of person who always *wants* a complicated dessert—an éclair, a canelé, a perfect crème brûlée (really, anything with an accent over the "e"). But I'm not going to do all that. So I settled for a cupcake. A dozen cupcakes.

Like a lot of people in their twenties, I had kitchen supplies that would get the job done but weren't quite the right thing. A misshapen plastic bowl, a spoon that was a little too big, an oven that was a little too small. I was in the process of saving up for a stand mixer, but it was very slow going because I had no money whatsoever, so I made the cupcakes and icing by hand.

At the end, the kitchen counter was covered in flour and buttercream smears and the sink was full of dishes, but I had my cupcake. It was all I wanted.

I was in a phase of life that was, in retrospect, typical of one's late twenties—money troubles, underemployment, the dawning thought, *Wait, is life a scam, lol?* I'd moved to Philadelphia in 2005, following a dream of finding success in the city's vibrant arts scene; now I was six years in and no closer to my goal. I was scrounging together money from odd jobs, then later as a legal assistant at a firm that was an hour away and barely netted me rent. I had had a friend breakup with my longtime roommate—it was my fault—and moved into a house with a gregarious guy I'd just met and his two cats, who were convinced I'd usurped their hanging-out room and who conducted *Mission: Impossible*–style break-ins at all hours of the day and night. The cats' names were Cole Hamels and Chase Utley, after two Phillies players, but I knew I'd never remember that, so I redubbed them Jennifer Hudson and Susan Sarandon. Both Oscar winners!

When I came to the city, I wanted to write for a living, I wanted to find love, I wanted to make peace with myself after some failures in college, I wanted to feel hope. Now all I wanted was a cupcake. So I made a cupcake. And it made me feel better.

Then, I kept making cupcakes. Directionless and with a dwindling social circle, I was soon making cupcakes multiple times a week. For no one!

My roommate was a bodybuilder, so I just want you to imagine the psychological terrorism of having every surface in a kitchen covered by baked goods when you're counting macros. But I was a man possessed. I tried out different flavors. Peanut butter icing on banana cakes. Strawberry icing on ginger cakes. Chocolate cakes with cherries in the center, topped with cream cheese icing. Rainbow Pride cupcakes that resulted in every dish in the kitchen being stained with dyes of different colors.

These were *creative* cupcakes, but they were not *impressive* cupcakes. Still, I kept making them. I made hundreds, perhaps thousands, of cupcakes. No one asked why. I don't hold this against anyone. Why are you looking at cupcakes and asking why? What are you, a philosopher?

Besides, baking wasn't a cry for help. I've done plenty of things before and since that are absolutely cries for help: dyeing my hair, abruptly moving to a different state, writing and publishing personal essays. But the cupcakes weren't that. They were, like the name of a cute shop in a Lifetime holiday movie, Just Desserts. I was in an unhappy phase of life that I feared I would never get out of, but baking didn't save me, either. Otherwise, this book would be called *Knead, Pray, Love* and have recipes in it and maybe there'd be two hands on the cover clapping in a cloud of flour. Oh, wouldn't that be nice?! Wouldn't that be lovely. Oh wow.

Anyway! There are no recipes in this book. If you want a recipe, google "cupcake recipes," because this part, my cupcake days, is just about over.

I baked for a couple of years as the other wants in my life stagnated. But surrounded by my sea of baked goods, my life unchanged, my belly full, I wondered what I was supposed to do once the cake was finished.

As an aspiring artist, I was used to taking every one of my interests and entrusting them with my financial well-being, but I never wanted to turn the cupcakes into a moneymaking endeavor. I was not going to become a cupcake professional. I was happy making something just for the pleasure of doing it. Family members were giving me restaurant-size vanilla and specialty baking tins for Christmas and birthdays; cupcakes became "my thing," but at the end of the day, it was a hobby. As I tried to make something of the rest of my life, I wondered if hobbies were a reflection of a deeper truth about the self or a diversion from it.

Throughout this period, my father would regularly come

across articles about 401(k)s and constructing one's five-year plan and send them to me, often on LinkedIn. Then I'd have to figure out what my LinkedIn password was, find my messages, and download an article my father had taken the time to scan in on his work computer. The PDFs would instruct me to map out an idea of what my future would look like, and I'd stare at them as if I was trying to decipher hieroglyphics. I knew what five-year plans were, but I didn't know how to begin making one for myself.

One of the ways I understand my father is as a businessman. There are a lot of businesspeople in the world, usually in airports. They have important jobs that I can't comprehend, and they take conference calls I can't follow. They know what the plan is. My father had the title of manager at a succession of companies and was now general-managing a public market. I love business words: "arbitrage," "circle back," "Excel!" What fun! But I thought that business was a component of an ordered universe I wasn't a part of.

Still, I read those LinkedIn messages with great interest. Not only were they talking about conceiving of myself outside my current circumstance, but they seemed to be just slightly beyond what the platform was built for. See, I saw LinkedIn as a place where things I knew nothing about happened—success, achievement, vision. But my father used those messages in the same way my parents always communicated to me: as a means of tapping into a deep well of encouragement. In those messages, he showed up fully as himself, which is a beautiful surprise to see on a website dedicated to endorsing one's colleagues' PowerPoint skills. He would also frequently send me "happy birthday" messages on LinkedIn, which I thought was lovely and idiosyncratic. Those five-year-plan messages seemed, at

first, to be quixotic assignments I couldn't do. But I kept looking and I saw another message underneath.

It said: "I see you. The future is coming. Keep going."

The five-year plan was "hope."

I made my way through hopeless years, one dozen cupcakes at
a time. Eventually, I met someone, we moved in together, and
he bought me a Vitamix, because I was all about juicing now.
My cupcake days were over. I got new jobs; I started freelance
writing on the side. My boyfriend and I broke up. I nearly
drowned in sorrow and juice. A year later I wrote a one-man
show about a search for God, a boyfriend, and baked goods. I
took unglamorous production photos of me eating a cupcake,
which I absolutely would not allow to be published today. In the
audience, I met a white social-justice-seeking pastor named
David. We got married a few weeks before the 2016 election,
which was an emotional whiplash–inducing series of events.
Two months later, I got laid off from my job but miraculously
managed to secure a full-time position at *ELLE.com*. I went to
visit their Manhattan offices for the first time and there were
fancy cupcakes waiting. I ate half of one.

My cupcake days seemed so far behind me then. I knew who
I was. I knew where I was going. I remembered my LinkedIn
password. Life was going the way I hoped. And then everything
changed. By 2017, I found myself living back in my hometown
after twelve years away, a stranger to myself, a stranger in my
marriage, unsure of what the plan was. I wanted to pull my
new stand mixer out, but my doctor was like, "You're getting
too old to have all that sugar, babe."

So, what now? What do you do when you find yourself in

cupcake days again and you're not in your twenties? What if you're nearly forty? What if you're sending a kid off to college? What if you're about to retire? I wondered if I'd missed the part of life that I'd been working toward. And there's a relief in that, I guess. You are freed from wanting something so badly and fearing that you won't get it or won't appreciate it or that you'll lose it too quickly. You can find contentment. But I wasn't content. And I wanted so much more than a cupcake.

Over the five years that followed, I would experience incredible highs that would transform me and crushing lows that would send me wandering into a wilderness. I'd change jobs, my husband and I would buy a house, we'd lose a parent, we'd search for community, all against the backdrop (and frequent foreground) of political upheaval and pandemic. None of this was in the plan.

But between the best days of life and the worst days of life, between what you thought your life would be and what it is, between two people, there is a vivid and strange expanse in the middle. This is the middle.

Part One

HOMECOMING

This Is Wudder

The appeal of the building was that it had an infinity pool and that it was situated next to the Jones Falls, a bucolic eighteen-mile stream that runs through Baltimore along I-83. Those were the things they were selling. The apartments were handsomely designed, carved out of the shell of an old sailcloth factory that later made model trains and dolls that were at least 40 percent haunted. It was an award-winning green-energy building that had preserved many of the original features, like huge wooden beams that crisscrossed throughout the floors. There was a "common room" in the middle of the third floor that had a computer workstation, a big TV, and a few couches for gathering.

"Imagine yourself watching the Super Bowl here while drinking a nice cold beer!" the leasing agent declared to me and my husband, David, when our tour reached the common room. And then she just stared at me as I desperately tried to force my brain to generate any of those images. "There's also a gym you can use anytime, day or night," she said.

"Please," I replied, "I'm having an aneurysm."

The selling points, however, were the pool, which was only about the size of two picnic tables but apparently went on infinitely, and the Falls, which attracted herons and geese and provided a peaceful view augmented by the dulcet sounds of highway traffic.

"I could be happy here," I said to David, which is a deranged kind of promise but also just a statement of fact. It was 2017 and we were currently living in Philadelphia, where, as a matter of fact, I was incredibly happy. I hadn't lived in Baltimore for going on thirteen years at that point. I'd hightailed it to New York for college, but after dropping out, I crash-landed back at my parents' house. Those years in Baltimore had been hard. I waited tables at a comedy club humorlessly, I came out to myself and the world in lurching fits and starts, I accidentally got myself canceled writing for a local college's newspaper. The usual catastrophic coming-of-age.

At the time, HBO was shooting the television series *The Wire* in my parents' redlined neighborhood, which felt simultaneously glamorous and demoralizing. I put a placard outside my bedroom window that read "filming location for a modern American tragedy." My parents had gone to great lengths to create a world of possibility in our house when I was growing up, but the outside world of the neighborhood was resolutely without hope. Abandoned by avaricious landlords and the elected officials supposedly representing it, the neighborhood may have been defined onscreen by the pervasive influence of drugs and violence, but the real story was of a people who were never afforded any options. While living there after college, I struggled to craft a better narrative for myself, let alone the city. Was such a thing even possible for me—a Black college dropout, a gay man whose conservative religious upbringing promised damnation, a failure?

Moving away had given me the chance to write another narrative, but it had also calcified my complicated feelings about my hometown into an active grudge. Callously, I used to quip, "I don't want to move back to Baltimore even to be buried."

And while it feels silly to have a feud with a city for what are, largely, personal problems, quirks of temperament, and crises I created on my own with the help of structural oppression, I did frequently write emails to the mayor of Baltimore with the subject line "APOLOGIZE!"

But the mayor had yet to write back as I stood in a refurbished factory-turned-luxury-apartment building. I looked from my husband to the realtor to the sparkling water by the highway and considered starting a new chapter in a story I thought was finished. *It is possible that I'll be happy. Here.*

I'd moved to Philadelphia on a whim that turned out to be a good idea in retrospect, which is the only way I plan. The first couple of years were just as hard as Baltimore in my early twenties had been, because, shockingly, riding two hours up I-95 did not bippity-boppity-boo me into some radically different person. But through trial and error, through pushing my boundaries, through the bippity-boppity of the passage of time, I found my people, and through them, I found a self that I liked.

Over the course of a decade and change, I had slowly and magically built a community, found artistic success, and met David, which are all promises they make to you in the Philadelphia constitution. The city motto is "Whiz Wit a Spouse," I believe. But by the summer after our wedding, we were at a turning point. I'd been laid off from a job at a university but had been lucky enough to have my freelance job writing a humor column for *ELLE.com* turn into a full-time gig. My career was stable but completely remote. David, meanwhile, had graduated from therapy school (like school to be a therapist, not that thing I do where I sign up for a writing workshop and just talk about my problems the whole time). He'd earned his second master's, his first being in divinity, but was having trouble finding a job as a pastor, which was his passion and his calling.

Pastors in the Presbyterian church have an internal job-search site where they upload a document called a Pastoral Information Form, or a PIF. The PIF gives details about your work history and training, as well as your interests, strengths, and biographical details. It's a little less Indeed.com than it is OkCupid, playing matchmaker between pastors and worshipping communities, the latter of which also fill out their own forms for open positions. In practice, it's like that one dating site where only women can make the first move. Pastors can submit their PIFs to open job positions, but the churches must initiate the interview process. (Okay, I know the way I'm describing this has you thinking, *Yeah, that's how jobs work,* but I assure you it's like dating. Each party is trying to make a commitment that will last years. Each party is trying to suss out something ineffable and far larger than themselves. Each party is placing their heart in the hands of the other. And it all starts with this little form.)

David had updated his PIF regularly and would come to me with news of potential churches in the area, but none of them were a match. They were good dates, but it wasn't love. I'd sit in our Philly apartment listening to him process the anxiousness of waiting to hear back from churches, feeling like Samantha on *Sex and the City* listening to Miranda talk about dates with anyone who wasn't Steve. I'd swirl my martini and lean forward saucily, saying things like "Honey, tell that church to get off the cross, we need the wood. Is this helpful? I'm almost certain it's not. Anyway, I support you. Wow, this is much stronger than I intended it to be. How did they get their jobs done on that show? Having a martini on a weeknight after the age of twenty-five is a death sentence! I'm going to bed."

It was an anxious time. We needed two incomes and, more important, David needed to work. He needed to fulfill his purpose in life. He needed to fall in love with a church.

So he was excited when a small, social-justice-focused congregation in a wooded area responded to his PIF. And he was elated when they invited him down to give a guest sermon, the pastoral dating equivalent of meeting the parents. And he was thrilled when they asked him to make it Facebook official, David and this little church in suburban Maryland, just outside of Baltimore, my former home.

There was no future that we considered where David wouldn't take the job. It just didn't make sense to turn it down simply because I had a toxic relationship with an entire metropolitan area. Like, get some help, Eric! The upside was, of course, that I had parents, one brother, and a sister-in-law in Baltimore and we'd get to see them more. The downside was that Baltimore was where all the ghosts of the unhappy person I used to be still lived.

"You're going to love your life here," the realtor promised us in the factory apartments.

"We'll take it," I replied. "But if you're wrong, prepare to receive an email from me. I will cc the mayor."

The factory was originally one long, rectangular, intermittently haunted building with a corridor of large dormer windows running down the middle of the roof. They were calling the wide space between the windows a clerestory now and had chopped up the building such that the clerestory was the top level of the fourth floor's apartments, with the bottom level having no windows at all. You opened the front door of the apartment to complete darkness, which led to a laundry room and a bathroom and the two bedrooms at the back. A staircase brought you to the kitchen/dining area on the clerestory level, which had floor-to-ceiling windows along its two longest walls. The clerestory was an open space with a wall of appliances and cabinets, the omnipresence of the sun, and the biggest, most gorgeous reclaimed-wood kitchen island I have ever seen.

Now here *I can be happy,* I thought.

Yes, this apartment was basically a greenhouse plopped on top of a bunker. Yes, the wooden beams that I wanted to use as bookshelves still had factory soot on them. Yes, the website advertised the building as "an escape from its Baltimore surroundings," which is kind of saying the quiet part out loud. Yes, "escape" is doing a lot of work here, as in "Are you trying to do white flight but in the bike lane? Look no further!" Yes, it was far more expensive than we'd budgeted and yet still the most reasonable choice in the market.

There were a few downsides.

But I could be happy with this Nancy Meyers kitchen island next to the Jones Falls, in an apartment with two floors, each of which had an aggressively distinct temperature.

When we'd driven down to look for apartments, I'd stared out the window at the city that I knew, many places unchanged in the years I'd been gone. As is my wont, I launched into stories prompted by the memories that got called up. And, as David would later inform me, every single story was the saddest thing he'd ever heard in his entire life. "Did you know that all of your stories about Baltimore are unhappy?" he asked. I was like, "*WHAT?*" This was legitimately shocking to me. I thought I was just adding color commentary to our rides. But it was true that the commentary included things like "Oh! That's where I was in an attempted carjacking! Oh! There's where my grandmother's funeral was. Oh! There's where my other grandmother's funeral was. The pastor said something shady about why we were having it on a weekday and not a weekend, and although I'm certain he's dead now, I'm still furious about it. Oh! This is where a cab driver threw me out of his cab because he was afraid to go to my neighborhood. That happened all the time. Oh! That's the Cheesecake Factory. Nothing bad happened there. Wait, no, they did fire me from the host stand."

I didn't know what to do with this observation from David. I know that you can look at your story from several vantage points, you can choose where to begin, where to end, and all that. But I don't think you can change the facts. And if the facts are unhappy, don't blame me. Blame the Cheesecake Factory circa 2002.

David's new church was going to pay for relocation, and David found a moving company that fit the price point and specialized in moving clergy. Most clergy come with large libraries, I was informed, and so these companies were adept at moving all the household items as well as, like, the Shroud of Turin and a bunch of books. We did, indeed, have a bunch of books in our combined library. David's were clergy stuff, God matters, the Book of Life. Mine were many copies of *The Pelican Brief* by John Grisham. It's a very good book.

The moving company had a website full of glowing reviews and promised three expert movers who would also professionally pack your stuff. I'd never used movers or packers before, so it was especially thrilling to step into the phase of life where I didn't have to test the bonds of a friendship by offering a pizza in exchange for struggling up a staircase with one of nine hundred poorly taped boxes. This was the life you lived when you had a Nancy Meyers kitchen island near the stream. This was the new Baltimore story for me!

This is the new Baltimore story for me, I thought again, with a different inflection, around 6 P.M. on moving day as I lay on my back in the furniture-less clerestory and stared up at the sky through the wall of windows. We had started the moving day in Philly at eight in the morning; David and I had arrived in Baltimore at 5 P.M., the movers following behind us. But, as David was discovering from a phone call, their truck had broken down on the highway and they had no idea when they or any of our belongings would arrive.

Things were not ideal.

Hours went by; 6 P.M. turned to 9 P.M. No movement on the truck. My mother came by with Boston Market for dinner. She'd picked up paper plates at the grocery store, since all our plates and clothes and copies of *The Pelican Brief* were sitting somewhere on I-95. She offered to let us crash on one of the four pullout sofas in my parents' house, but we protested. We had to be here when our stuff arrived. Whenever that was.

She went home and told us to call her when the movers got there. I sat on the floor of the clerestory, eating Boston Market macaroni and cheese from a paper plate that read "Happy Birthday." It was no one's birthday, which I found even more enjoyable. All in all, it was kind of a lovely evening—gorgeous place, lots of space. I'd accidentally Marie Kondo'd my entire life, and, you know what, she's got a point. Plus, I got to eat an objectively good mac and cheese. I don't think it risks my Black card to admit this. Boston Market mac and cheese is good. It's very good! Wonderfully flavorful European-American mac. Congratulations to the city of Boston. Congratulations to Chef Ben Affleck.

David called the movers around 10 P.M. We were exhausted. We asked them if we could get them a hotel room to stay in and we'd try again in the morning. They told us that tomorrow was their day off. We begged them. "Please, this is crazy! We have neighbors who are trying to 'escape' from Baltimore; we can't be thumping and bumping in the middle of the night like the Watergate burglars." The movers held fast; they were coming. I mean, actually, they weren't. They were just sitting somewhere. But they weren't *not* coming. So. Alert Woodward and Bernstein.

It also came out that only one of them worked for the company and the other two were just guys from Craigslist. Which, well, tracks considering that when they'd arrived, they seemed flummoxed by the prospect of packing our apartment and had spent the day wandering around holding tall wardrobe boxes, tossing in our belongings with no apparent system.

Things weren't going well, baby!

What's amazing in retrospect (my go-to form of 'specting) is that although we were actively in the process of being scammed (the website reviews turned out to be fake; they tried to charge us more money than we'd agreed to; none of the movers were professionally trained or insured in any way), the issue at hand was just bad luck. I love to have an attempted bamboozling interrupted by fate, the ultimate scam goddess. These guys, who'd stared bewildered at our apartment as if they'd never seen a human dwelling before, were as screwed as we were.

I licked cheese sauce off a celebratory paper plate and thought, *What if I leave it all behind? Who needs my stuff?*

What if it never arrives and I simply . . . start over? Or embrace extreme minimalism. Downsize to nothingness. Make my motto "My ana-Kondo don't want none!" I felt free! Well, actually, I felt delirious with fatigue and I'm pretty sure I'd reached the bargaining stage, but whatever. Why be negative? I was telling a new story. I was like Miranda Priestly in *The Devil Wears Prada:* I worked for a fashion magazine, I wondered why no one was ready, and I had no use for "a pile of stuff."

I didn't share my new level of enlightenment with David. He's sentimental; I was sure he was still about that stuff life. Couldn't chance it. When we'd moved in together, I'd been struck by the care and thoughtfulness he put into holding on to memories, mementos, people, and the past. He had family heirlooms, souvenirs from his childhood, college, and travels abroad, all of which came with a story, and only rarely were those stories the saddest thing I had ever heard. Remarkable. In that way he reminded me of my mother, whose scrapbooks fill every surface in my old bedroom, whose photos number in the hundreds of thousands, and whose work to piece together our family tree has bridged time and space. For David and for my mom, histories are lifelines and sources of joy and understanding. Leaving them behind is the worst possible outcome.

If I was being honest, I'd admit that I didn't want to leave *everything* behind. Indeed, mere hours earlier, David and I had sat on the front stoop of the Philly brownstone where we'd been so happy, watching the double-parked moving truck to make sure it didn't get towed. Because we'd been on Broad Street for literally the entire day, we'd seen a huge cross-section of the city pass by. And many of those people, as happens when you've lived many lives for over a decade in a city, were people that we knew and liked and loved. It was as if our going-away party had been a street festival. It was a truly beautiful day. I never wanted it to end. We'd gotten to say goodbye or see you later or do you remember when. And I carried it with me down the highway. I had been so happy and somehow, somewhere, *that* was in the moving truck, too. In the grains of sand clinging to our beach mat from a recent group trip or in the place cards and tea lights from our wedding or in the ticket stubs and programs I'd dutifully saved from nights out at the theater. (Oh God, was *I* sentimental, too?!)

Okay, fine, I like the happy memories and I want to hold on to them. And, *sure,* there were a couple of things in that truck that I wouldn't mind holding on to. It was just that for a moment I thought that I could be completely new, even in Baltimore, where I was so old. I could, like the website promised, escape.

I used to be a messy person—I'm talking specifically about leaving piles of things everywhere, but, yes, I was also messy in the sense that I was emotionally chaotic, made terrible life choices, and sometimes started drama. But right now we're talking about stuff. As my life got better, however, I'd become very anticlutter. I romanticized professors' homes filled with books and Nora Ephron characters who had New York apartments crammed with knickknacks, but I felt like *my* clutter was a cry for help. It wasn't cute clutter; it was mess. I wanted to project, if not emotional stability, emotional cuteness. No wagon-wheel coffee table for me! After David and I moved in together, the question that always arose in our house was, "Is this clutter or is this a treasured personal artifact that Eric is heartlessly trying to donate to Goodwill?" It was a process. But at this point in my life, I wanted to be in a space with less stuff. And physically I was already there, in that empty Nancy Meyers kitchen with the stainless-steel side-by-side fridge (my first!) and the reclaimed-wood island so big that Huck and Big Jim could sail on it down the Mississippi. (You may be asking yourself why the hell I used *that* example? Are there no other rafts in all of pop culture? Of course there are, but *I'm a messy person!*)

I loved the new apartment bare. My favorite design aesthetic is "No one lives here." I had friends with money, usually white friends, whose places looked like a West Elm showroom. All the construction elements were new, all the furniture was pristine mid-century modern, and there wasn't a sock or a box of tissues or a family photo as far as the eye could see. These people never seemed to have belongings. Where is the stack of the papers you wrote in college? Where are your souvenir hurricane glasses from a Hard Rock Cafe in Las Vegas? Where is the blanket your grandmother made you that doesn't match anything? It was a frictionless kind of life, it seemed, where only the present existed. That was so attractive to me, someone who had always lived in old houses, someone who was surrounded by dust, someone whose past was all friction.

But the clerestory was new. Well, no, it wasn't, either. There was century-old soot on the bookshelves. It looked new, though.

Around midnight, David got another update from the immobile movers: The company was sending a new truck. They were going to unload everything from the old truck into the new truck and then the company was sending a truck tow truck and they were going to drive the new truck and tow the old truck to our apartment. Like a riddle.

Years earlier, my parents rented a U-Haul to get my stuff from our house in Baltimore to college in New York. Somehow I managed to fill the whole box truck, despite being an actual child with no belongings save for a gigantic Dell computer and an extensive collection of original-cast albums on CD. I'd felt an initial pang of embarrassment seeing my classmates, who I assumed were chic characters, dropping only a few boxes into the big red moving bins. I felt, already, weighed down by who I was.

It didn't exactly help my feelings of otherness that, while my belongings covered more than half of the space in my room, my roommate grew up two blocks from campus and had moved in by bringing a backpack and a snake in an aquarium. The basics. Out in the dorm common area, I met a suitemate, said one sentence to him, and he physically jumped back and cried, "Whoa, why do you talk like that? Where the hell are you from?"

Honey, when I tell you I was *shocked*. I felt so exposed and confused. I was immediately clockable in a way that I hadn't even thought through. The suitemate was, it turned out, from Baltimore County, so maybe what I mistook for judgment was actually kinship, but it didn't feel like it then. The disorientation of that moment never left me. Here I was, living the first day of my new New York story, with all my baggage out in the street.

I really didn't think I had an accent. And I still generally identify myself as a Not Having Accent American. And I certainly didn't have a *Baltimore* accent. If you were listening to this on audiobook, you might have heard that last statement and gone, "Now, sis . . ." But I stand by this. The Baltimore accent is a specific and intense little creature. Or, I should say, the white Baltimore accent. White Baltimoreans historically have a vaguely Southern marble-mouthed style of speech that elongates "ohs" into "ohhwwwws," as in "rohhwwwm" instead of "roam," and flattens "ahhs" into "uhhhs," as in "wudder" instead of "water," and shrinks up words like "mayor" into "mere." It's an accent that feels like a tight jaw and loose lips. It's hard to explain or imitate unless it comes naturally. John Travolta attempted it in *Hairspray*, a noble effort, and my icon Kathy Bates tried . . . something in *American Horror Story: Freak Show*. The ex-cent huz taken dohwwn e'en the greats, hohn!

Black Baltimoreans have a very different accent. It's quicker, more musical, and comes from higher in the face. There's still a bit of marble mouth, but maybe the marbles are smaller? I don't know. I'm not a linguist. And I don't have an accent, no matter what you hear.

My unsuccessful attempts to hide harbingers of my hometown notwithstanding, as I stood on the side of the road at 1 A.M., watching the truck and the tow truck and all of our belongings pull up, I had to admit I was having an unmistakably Baltimore move. All Baltimoreans have relocation trauma. It's our core wound, even those of us with fraught relationships to the city itself. In 1984—I'm sorry, I'm getting choked up just thinking about this—the owner of the Baltimore Colts, the city's football team at the time, hired the Mayflower moving company to pack up the team's offices in Baltimore in the middle of the night and secretly move the Colts to their new home in Indianapolis. Where they reside *to this day*. The city woke up to find that their football team had been straight-up Grinched! The Mayflower moving company was unofficially blacklisted for years in various neighborhoods in the city. Folks were rending their garments in the streets. And even though I was but a toddler when this happened and I do not care about football, I am still going to claim this trauma.

Because our moving trucks were too big to fit into the garage, the movers were going to have to unload everything onto the side of the dark, winding, wooded road. It was like we were being reverse broken up with. While they unloaded, David and I carried boxes the length of the garage, up the elevator, back down the length of the building, and into the apartment. Over and over. All night.

We finally finished at six in the morning. The sun was coming up, glinting off the Jones Falls. The movers left, off to scam elsewhere. David and I walked into our bunker and greenhouse, now choked with boxes and dust. We were *so* tired, so beaten. All we wanted to do was sleep. I don't think we even put together the bed frame. We just needed sheets. And it was then that we realized how little these randos from Craigslist knew about packing. None of the boxes were labeled beyond the room they came from, and when we opened them, we discovered there was no wrapping, no care, no order at all to the contents. It was just stuff.

We dug through boxes, searching for anything that looked like the wreckage of our linen closet. Finally, I found them. They were in a tall wardrobe box with levels of different kinds of belongings. The top level was shoes. All our shoes. The next level down was our beach stuff, recently used on a trip. And underneath all that were our sheets.

I pulled out a set of sheets; they were covered in sand. I didn't care. I put them on the bed anyway. We lay down on the sand and went to sleep.

"Welcome home," David said.

"Welcome hohhwwm," I said.

Maybe Going Back Again

One time I went to get my eyebrows waxed because I was bored in life. I was in my late twenties, living in Philadelphia, and still in the uncomfortable process of becoming. Instead of blaming the city for my unease, however, I blamed my follicles. I love to find simple solutions for complex problems.

I'd read in a magazine that when you get your eyebrows done, you should bring in a photo of someone whose eyebrows you want. I literally had never thought about it. I don't tend to notice eyebrows. The only eyebrows I could call to mind were Bert's from *Sesame Street*. I googled a picture of him and printed it out. Suspecting that this was not sufficient preparation, I then searched "celebrity eyebrows." Beloveds, this is not a useful thing to do with your time. You get a bunch of before-and-after photos of people like Gwen Stefani and Angelina Jolie who went from having the pencil-thin arched eyebrows that were popular in the early 2000s to a fuller, more rounded shape that's popular now.

Then I asked myself, *Who do you want to look like?* This is always tricky, because my brain comes back with answers like *Prince, Julia Roberts, the handsome guy from spin class.* And then I'm like, *Brain, you gotta get it together. Let's work with what's achievable.* And my brain is like, *Alas, that is not one of my core competencies. We're trying to fix internal issues using body wax.*

I don't really know who I want to look like, because I absolutely do not have a clear idea of what I actually look like. I just looked in the mirror before writing this; every single pertinent detail of my face has already left my mind. I could not pick myself out of a lineup. I am serious. If you brought me a police sketch artist and asked me to describe myself, you'd get a picture of Angelina Jolie accepting the Oscar for *Girl, Interrupted.* Do other people forget what they look like a lot? I'll see a photo of myself and think, *Who is that man? And why is he frowning? Oh! He should get his eyebrows done!*

I went back to the drawing board with the eyebrow search. I tried to think of celebrities with similar skin tones and face shapes to mine. I immediately googled Jesse Williams, the hot biracial doctor with light eyes from *Grey's Anatomy.* Intellectually, I know I don't look a *thing* like Jesse Williams, but every time I'm prompted to say my celebrity doppelgänger, I always confidently announce, "Jesse Williams, one of the most attractive men in the world." I guess I don't understand the difference between "celebrity doppelgänger" and "everyone's crush." I kept searching. I came upon a photo of Vin Diesel. Maybe you don't know this, but he has nice eyebrows. And he's bald, like I am. Basically twins. I printed that one out. Somehow my search of Vin Diesel images also produced a random photo of Halle Berry. She has wonderful eyebrows. I printed that out, too.

I walked into a nail salon, sat down in the wax chair, and handed the technician a photo of Bert, a photo of Vin, and a photo of Halle. I left the Jesse Williams photo at home. I was being reasonable. She looked at the photos like I'd given her a bill from the IRS.

"These are some guide images for you," I said, pointing helpfully to my own eyebrows. She scowled at me and threw the photos in the trash.

"Never do this again," she said.

And I still don't know if she meant never bring in photos, never delude yourself about what you look like, or never doubt that you're perfect just the way you are, my sweet darling.

I've been told I have one of those faces that looks like somebody. I don't know who that somebody is, which is kind of a larger existential question. But people often will tell me, while staring at me with an expression of utter confusion, "You look like someone . . ." Strangers in Philly would always stop me and swear we'd met. This is before I was in any way googleable. I was just some poorly dressed paralegal. But, also, I was somebody.

When this would happen, I'd suggest maybe I waited on them at Hard Rock Cafe or perhaps they frequented the storytelling show I'd started attending, but that was never the case. "You *look* like somebody!" they'd say.

I would say, "Is this a metaphor?"

They would say, "Shh, I'm thinking."

Eventually, one of us would give up. In these instances, as with most awkward social situations, the whole thing always drags on too long and everybody knows it and the person who disengages first is a true hero. I learned to say, "I have one of those faces that looks like someone's cousin," which maybe feels flippant or a sly reference to "All Black folk look alike," but people tend to accept it nonetheless. I meant it as a small joke; however, it's totally plausible. A good portion of my mother's extended family lives in Philadelphia. So it's conceivable that the cousin I look like may be my own.

I've also noticed that a lot of the Black folk I encounter in the Mid-Atlantic region remind me of people I know or I am related to or I got introduced to once at a barbecue. I'm sure there's a sociological reason for it, relating to the Great Black Migration. But I don't know how to get the answer. And every time I go to a library and ask, "Can you point me to books that would tell me why I look like someone's cousin?" they seem distressed. It probably doesn't help that I'm usually clutching a photo of Halle Berry.

Oddly enough, when we moved back to Baltimore, people stopped telling me I looked like somebody. That was not what I expected, especially considering I'd grown up there and gone to school, church, celebrity look-alike contests at the state fair there. I presumed people would keep mistaking me for an idea they couldn't quite grasp. Or, more likely, they would just recognize me. Instead, no one came up to me at all.

About a year after we moved, I went to a homegoing service in Baltimore at our old church with my parents and my youngest brother, Jeffrey. The service was for a dear friend of our family. I hadn't set foot inside that church in over twenty years, but I loved the woman who had passed and I loved her family.

I stood in the aisle before the service, next to my parents and Jeffrey, as people arrived, milled about, and greeted each other. A lot of people we knew at the church had left in the last two decades, and so this was a sad sort of reunion for many in attendance. I was totally disoriented—the church looked exactly the same, down to the homemade banners that hung behind the altar. And the faces I was seeing looked almost the same, except in some cases with a little gray hair or the hint of a wrinkle. Honestly, it looked like that thing in movies where someone in their thirties is wearing old-age makeup. That's how I remembered most of these people—as the thirty- and forty-year-old friends of my parents. Now here I was, thirty-seven myself. I didn't believe what I was seeing was real. I felt like I'd stepped back twenty years but everyone was trying to pretend time had moved on.

As if that wasn't strange enough, people that I'd grown up with, looking like they'd just stepped out of the hair-and-makeup trailer for a flash-forward on *This Is Us*, would come over, greet my parents warmly, say hello to Jeffrey, and then extend their hand to me and welcome me to the church as if it was my first time. Honestly, they were like, "Hello, sir, so glad you could join us today. Are you saved?" It wasn't everyone. Others came up and greeted me with warmth; some even asked about David. But enough people approached me like a total stranger that I was like, "Is this shade?" I would have respected that. But no; they really didn't know who I was! I would tell them, "It's me! Eric! Standing here next to my parents, whom I resemble, and my brother, also in the same genetic neighborhood." And their eyes would widen and their mouths would fall open and they'd say, "Eric?! I didn't even recognize you!"

Maybe it was the eyebrows.

Sometimes, I'd wonder who it was that I wanted anyone to recognize. I considered myself a new version of me, after all, albeit a new version who kept seeing the ghosts of the people I used to be. One of the ways I convinced myself that I was changing when I was in Philadelphia was through others' perceptions of me, be they trusted friends or eyebrow waxers. But the experience in Baltimore felt more isolated. I felt dimensionless.

I would drive around the city, telling myself the weird sad stories that I used to tell David. Adding new weird, sad stories to the bunch. "Oh! This is the church where no one knew me, like a parable or a *Twilight Zone* episode."

One night I went to the Charles, an independent movie theater that I've always loved and that had, for years, expanded my world and made me feel more at home in my skin. There's nothing like watching a matinee of a soul-crushing Lars von Trier movie at the age of twenty-two, while hideously depressed, to make you feel alive. I was early for my film that night, so I stopped into the tapas restaurant next door. I love how every time you go to a tapas place in America, they explain the concept of tapas to you. It never fails to sound like the complicated rules of a network-TV game show. "The plates are going to come out whenever. You're going to order a bunch of them. We refuse to accept only one answer. We're just going to toss solitary meatballs out of the kitchen at you like Skee-Ball. At some point your table will have upwards of twenty dishes on it. We are not responsible for structural damage." Tapas-style eating makes sense; it's like having a personal buffet—what's not to love? But every server who has ever approached my table makes it sound like an unsuccessful pitch on *Shark Tank*.

I sat at the bar and braced myself for the barrage of tapas-related non sequiturs ("A plate smaller than the eye can see, if you can believe it, Sharks!"), but instead, the bartender came over, poured me a glass of rosé, and immediately started talking about "the schedule" and how it had changed since I left. This was a style of tapas with which I was not familiar.

When it was time for my movie, I went to pay for my drink, but the bartender just laughed and said, "Get out of here!" It was either kind or rude. I still don't know!

A few weeks later, I went to the Italian restaurant in the bottom floor of our apartment building. We'd been a couple of times for happy hour, but this time I was alone and there was a bartender I didn't know. She brightened when she saw me, poured me a glass of rosé, and winked at me. I was used to special treatment because I look like Jesse Williams, but it was still curious. When she finished with another guest, I waved her over. I didn't know exactly how to phrase my question, so I said, "Why is wine?" She looked at me quizzically. I tried again. "I don't mean to sound weird but . . . do I look like someone?"

As it turned out, there was a sommelier who had been incredibly popular in Baltimore, had worked all over, loved rosé, and had recently moved to a different city. And, according to the bartender, the sommelier and I favored each other. Finally, I once again looked like somebody. And this was actually a Somebody.

"Do I have to pay for this wine?" I asked.

A few weeks later, I was seeing another film at the Charles, so I again had a pre-show glass of wine at the tapas restaurant. The bartender produced a rosé almost before I could sit down. Then he told me he was super swamped but he was happy to see me. And then he was gone. Did I walk in thinking I'd get a free glass of wine? Who can say? I'm not an expert on human nature! I'm just a person trying to understand how small the plates are. Should I have told the bartender before he poured me the glass that I wasn't who he thought I was? I'm not one to mansplain.

Did I, if ever so briefly, feel at home in a life where people recognized me, remembered me, and were happy to see me? Even if I wasn't the me they were trying to see?

The following summer was my twentieth high school reunion, and I was eager to go someplace where I knew I existed. At that point I'd been back in Baltimore for nearly two years, and I'd started to make inroads in finding community. But more often than not I still felt like I was in a *Twilight Zone* episode. I had been looking forward to my class reunion for a long time, which, given the strange personal choices that I've just detailed, probably makes me sound like one of those guys whose best self was his high school version and who, having peaked then, is always talking about "getting the gang back together!" But that's not true in my case, because in high school I was also weird. I don't wish I'd peaked in the past, but there is a certain relief in that, right? You know how things are going to play out. There's less about which to be anxious. Just fifty to sixty years of vibing. Not the worst.

A lot of my old friends weren't planning on coming to the reunion, because they hadn't loved their high school experiences, and I totally got that. I really liked my school, an independent K–12 that I'd attended from fourth grade on, but I wasn't trying to go back and relive some glory days. Imagine me walking the halls asking teenagers, "Do they still talk about that production of *Little Shop of Horrors* from 1998 where the voice of the plant was just superb?" I didn't want to be the main character of the reunion, but I wouldn't hate the opportunity to reckon with the past. What is a class reunion, after all, if not a chance to let the people that knew you when you were unfinished know that you'd somehow gotten it together in the end?

Mostly, though, I was going because I like stories—I wanted to see how some stories were continuing. I wanted a little bit of nostalgia, sure, but mostly I was interested in the inherent drama that reunions promise. We're a bunch of strangers, some of whom did not get along twenty years ago, and now you're going to put us in a room together with an open bar, heavy hors d'oeuvres, and no agenda save for whatever we didn't get to in therapy? It's not a reunion; it's dinner theater!

David and I took a Lyft out to the school, which brought back memories of riding in the back seat of my parents' cars up I-83 during morning car pool. I asked the driver to play a mix of the soundtrack to the underrated movie *The Five Heartbeats* and some nineties gospel to complete the mood. The first event of the night was an all-classes social hour. The school invites classes celebrating milestone years to the alumni weekend, but any alumni are welcome at the social hour, so it was a broad mix of people ranging from twenty-something to seventy-something, all congregating in a new wing built on top of an area where the swing sets used to be. I walked in and declared to no one in particular, "Call me Madonna, cuz this used to be my playground."

I found some familiar faces in the crowd. One guy from my class who I didn't really know that well but was friendly with struck up a conversation, but it went nowhere because we were both sort of half updating each other and half just stating random facts like we were in an experimental play. At one point, he said, "You went to Harvard."

I said, "No, I was wait-listed at Harvard. I'm still expecting to hear back."

"I was sure you went to Harvard," he replied.

"Do you think about this a lot?" I asked.

He said, "Am I confusing you with someone else?"

I said, "I don't think so." And then I listed all the people in our class who had gotten into Harvard, because that's still information that's sitting in my head.

My graduating class was small, about ninety students, so we were all up in each other's business all the time. Many of us later followed each other on Facebook, so we continued to be up in each other's business. I think this is another reason some people chose not to come back for the reunion. The event wasn't promising grand reveals or chance encounters with someone you'd only seen across a huge lecture hall. None of us were truly strangers; we were just older.

A guy came up to me, looking excited. I realized in that instant that I'd had a huge crush on him back in the day. I hadn't realized it was a crush at the time because I was not in touch with reality. And because we didn't really know each other. He was a secondary member of the jock royalty, as much as anyone can be a member of jock royalty in our slightly hippie-ish, liberal, progressive school on one hundred acres of woods with an Appalachian Challenge course. But the minute he called my name and I looked in his direction, I was suddenly thrown back in time, sitting in chemistry next to him and staring at his profile dreamily. And then I was back in the present, just grinning at this straight father of two (obviously I follow him on Facebook) and introducing him to my husband like, "This will come as a surprise, but I am gay now."

The guy I had chemistry with (Wait! I just got that!) was thrilled to see me, which was thrilling to me, as well. He said, "I saw one of your tweets in *Vogue*! Did you know that?"

I replied, "Um, I write a column for *ELLE*, so maybe that's what you're thinking of?"

He said, "It was *Vogue*! Did you know that?"

I said, "Perhaps!"

He went out to the patio to join the other members of the jock royalty. (I'm really leaning too heavily on the social-group distinction here. They were just people who played lacrosse and field hockey and soccer and some of them dressed cool by the standards of the time. They are fully three-dimensional people in life. Just not in this story.)

I turned to David. "I had such a crush on that guy!"

He said, "Yeah, that's pretty clear."

Then, like a sociopath, I pulled out my phone and tweeted, "I'm at my 20-year high school reunion. My crush is here!!!"

A little while later, a woman came up to me at the lamb empanadas station. She'd been a couple of years behind me, but we'd been friendly. She told me, "My wife really likes your column in *ELLE*." Finally, someone who had read my updated LinkedIn. She added, "My wife is also having a great time following your live tweets about the reunion."

So then I tweeted, "I've just found out that my classmate's wife is following my live tweets!" Here's me, just a Harvard-educated, surprisingly not-straight *Vogue* reporter, clutching a plate of parmesan bacon twists, a phone, and his youth.

I was having a wonderful time. And David was having a wonderful time. And I wasn't really sure what my objective was beyond that. I don't think I had anything to prove or disprove. Not to them, at least. I'd spent the last two decades mulling over every weird, embarrassing thing I did in high school, just like everyone does. But I'd also spent two decades building a self who wasn't ashamed of being weird or embarrassing or not fully knowing who he was or having a crush on a classmate that I didn't realize or act on in any way. Realizing the crush and realizing its obviousness, for instance, would have ruined my life back then, and now I was tweeting about it for the benefit of my friend's wife. I felt like myself at the reunion, in both the old way and the new way. I felt like myself for the first time in Baltimore.

After the social hour, we were split up to attend the class-specific reunions, which included dinner and an open bar. The class of 1999 reunion was in the cafeteria, and we arrived to find the bar in the center of the room and clusters of very nice couches in our respective spaces.

There was a tall table where the alumni office had laid out name tags for every member of our graduating class, whether they'd RSVP'd or not. Adorably, the tags had our senior yearbook photos printed on them. I searched for mine and I found, next to the name "Eric Thomas," a photo that looked like one of Tim the Tool Man Taylor's sons on *Home Improvement*. A white guy with blond hair that was split down the middle, as was the style back then. I knew that I'd changed a lot since high school, but still, I was like, "Something's . . . wrong here." It was the other Eric in my class, a nice guy who I was friends with and who hadn't come to the reunion. "No worries," I declared to no one. "They've just switched the Erics." I searched for his name. And I found . . . the same photo. Jonathan Taylor Thomas twice.

So, if you're keeping score at home, that's two Other Erics, zero Me Erics. I thought I was at the reunion, but it turns out that I was not! I immediately took a photo of the name tags and tweeted it so my friend's wife could be caught up.

I love the alumni office at my high school and have gone back to talk to classes and done events with them and donated, but I am very serious when I say someone should go to jail for this.

I didn't know what else to do, so I put the name tag with somebody else's face on my gay li'l sports coat and went to the bar.

"Do you think this is a metaphor?" I asked the bartender as she poured a free rosé that was actually for me.

Oh My, This Soup's Delicious, Isn't It?

There's a post from 2013 on the popular Facebook account Humans of New York that I think about a lot. In it, opera singer Steven Cole sits on a bench in Central Park; he's got one leg crossed over the other and leans back a bit from the camera, a wry smile on his lips. The caption, quoting him, says that Julia Child would have been 101 the week prior and he celebrates her birthday every year. "This year I cooked some smoky eggplant soup, and ate it in Central Park," he says.

The photographer, Brandon Stanton, asks, "Were you alone?"

"Of course," Cole answers. "I love to be alone. I'm fabulous." Okay, hello, *yes*. This is the energy that I'm trying to cultivate in my damn life, honey! I love his self-satisfaction and confidence. I love his commitment to ritual and to his own fabulousness. It's a testament to the pleasures of enjoying your own company, not despite whoever else is or isn't in your world, but because your own company is enough. Cole is the main character in his life, at least in this post. But I also think of his Julia Child ritual as possessing extraordinary sidekick energy. In some glorious, as-yet-unwritten sitcom, a chicly dressed character swans into an apartment to drop off a Tupperware container of smoky eggplant soup and deliver some choice bon mots. Then he slides back out the door, off to Central Park, because he doesn't want to keep his life or the spirit of Julia Child waiting.

In the city of my birth, in our new apartment full of half-unpacked boxes, I was trying to learn how to enjoy my own company, and the lessons weren't going so well. We'd been in Baltimore for six months; David's work kept him busy, his propensity to plan big and deliver big dovetailing with the kind of overwhelming flurry of activity that comes with starting a new job, especially a new job where the buck stops with you. (Well, technically, at a church, the buck stops with God, I guess. But is the Lord running payroll this week? No, God is busy. So you better fire up QuickBooks, buddy.)

My work at *ELLE* kept me busy during the day, plus I was writing and revising a proposal for what would eventually become my first book, *Here for It: Or, How to Save Your Soul in America* (now available in paperback!). But, in my cave-like den, writing internet comedy while Kelly Ripa and Ryan Seacrest told each other hilarious stories on mute on my TV, I began to wonder if I was maybe a bit lonely. It's quaint now to think of how novel and confusing working from home was to me during those first months in Baltimore in 2017 and early 2018.

Sometimes I would go to a coffee shop where everyone wore Carhartt jackets and the music on the record player was always perfect. I'd blast myself to Mars on caffeine and spend the day writing my column while intermittently tweeting deranged things about my favorite videos from the television show *Glee* (Top pick: Santana and Mercedes singing the Adele mash-up. The pinnacle of human creation. I will not debate this point).

But was sitting in the corner of a coffee shop, screaming at my internet friends, really being in the world? Did it stop the sinking feeling that I got when the coffee wore off and the shop closed and I drove back down Falls Road to my lonely top-floor apartment?

I decided I needed more resolve. I was a new person and these were new challenges and I needed to meet them head-on. I thought of Mrs. Peacock in *Clue,* who, finding herself at an awkward dinner with strangers where no one is talking, launches into a rambling speech. She wants to fill the silence, yes, but she, too, enjoys her own company, albeit in a far more chaotic way than Steven Cole described on Humans of New York. "Well, someone's got to break the ice," she declares, "and it might as well be me. I mean, I'm used to being a hostess, it's part of my husband's work. And it's always difficult when a group of new friends meet together for the first time, to get acquainted. So, I'm perfectly prepared to start the ball rolling. I mean, I . . . I have absolutely no idea what we're doing here. Or what I'm doing here. Or what this place is about. But I am determined to enjoy myself. And I'm very intrigued, and, oh my, this soup's delicious, isn't it?" *Perhaps I can be Mrs. Peacock,* I thought. I didn't have to be a passive participant in my life. I could be the host of it.

I started wandering the halls of the building during the day. No one was ever out and about on a constitutional. "I'm perfectly prepared to start the ball rolling," I'd call through closed doors. I started hanging out in the building gym, watching TV from one of the weight benches. "I have absolutely no idea what I'm doing here or what this place is about," I'd announce to the empty room.

David and I tried to make inroads with the other residents of the fourth floor by throwing a wine-and-cheese night in the third-floor common room. Two people came. "I'm used to being a hostess, it's part of my husband's work," I told them, trying to mask my disappointment. After an hour, one of the third-floor residents told us we were being too loud and we should leave. We were speaking at normal conversational volumes, and I'm still mad about it.

There was a cool couple down the hall—or at least I assumed they were cool; she had great hair; he wore band T-shirts. I'm not picky. But I only ran into them in the elevator sporadically, and they always seemed to be enjoying each other's company too much to bother with small talk. "Well, someone's got to break the ice!" I'd say as I walked into the elevator, grinning widely. They'd nod and go back to their conversation.

Agh, this soup. It's cold.

One Saturday morning, I was sitting in bed scrolling through Instagram, which is a great way to convince yourself that you're enjoying your own company. *I am entertaining myself by looking at the Instagram stories of my two thousand closest friends,* I'd tell myself. *It looks like they're having a lot of fun without me!*

"Looks like a lot of fun without me!" I commented on thirty different posts. I scrolled until I got hungry and decided that perhaps I should see what was happening in the world beyond my bedroom. Despite the fact that we'd been in the apartment for over half of a year, the chaotically packed boxes had proven to be too much of a mental barrier and we hadn't gotten to most of them, which meant that I had to shimmy through a narrow aisle to get to the closet and then basically guess where my clothes were. I threw on a pair of shorts, shimmied back, and tidied up a couple of glasses I'd left beside the bed out of laziness—two coffee mugs and three pint glasses for water. I really don't understand how my desk and my bed accumulate so many drink containers. I spend most of the time in bed asleep. Who is drinking?

The glasses in hand, I jogged upstairs to the kitchen. Midway up I stumbled, and the stacked water glasses bounced and shattered in my hand. I caught myself and saw that, in falling, I'd spilled grape juice all over the ecru carpet of the stairs. I stared for a second, trying to figure out where the grape juice had come from. And then I looked at my right arm, which, it turns out, had been ripped asunder by a piece of glass like a henchman in *Kill Bill*. I don't want to be too graphic about this, but blood was spraying everywhere and I was peering, curiously, at the inside of my own arm. My first thought was: *This is the grossest thing I've ever seen.* My second thought was: *Wow. Def gonna die.* Like, not to body-shame myself, but the interior of my body is disgusting. I was shocked by everything I was seeing, and I just kind of looked at it for a minute. *Yuck,* I thought. *Canceled.*

Having heard the noise, David came running around the corner, saw me looking like Carrie at the prom, and raced away to get a dish towel. As an Eagle Scout, he's very well trained in first aid. I am neither of those things, but I have a lot of opinions. I've found that when we're in emergency situations, we start to speak very loudly and very clearly to each other, as if we're both attempting to reach a frequency that overrides the other's neurosis. David shout-enunciated at me, "SIT DOWN. I DON'T WANT YOU TO FAINT. I'M GETTING GAUZE."

I shout-enunciated back, "THERE'S GLASS ON THE STAIRS! BE CAREFUL! I MAY HAVE GOTTEN BLOOD ON YOUR BOOK BAG."

He made me sit on the floor of the kitchen while he got more towels. I kept expecting to get freaked out by what was happening, but I wasn't. I found it all so fascinating and weird. I was just going along. I was a soup person! What a fun adventure for a Saturday. *This is going to make it hard to type today,* I thought. *And I have a box to unload; that's going to be annoying.* The dish towel started to drip. I thought, *Perhaps this is a problem.*

David appeared at the doorway of the kitchen again. I looked up at him and asked, "Do you think I should go to the hospital?"

"Of course you're going to the hospital!" he replied. The thought occurred to me that maybe I wasn't completely in my right mind. In retrospect, that was quite obvious. I'd lost a fair amount of blood, and I was just chilling on the floor, trying to figure out what errands I needed to run. Baby, I was in outer space. It was wonderful! *Is this what drugs are like?*

David guided me downstairs and went to get me some shoes. "Hold your arm above your heart," he called.

"Yesterday was shoulder day, so I'm a little sore actually," I said, as I wandered into the bathroom, still dripping blood. I started rummaging through the medicine cabinet, looking for my multivitamin. I'd forgotten to take it and it seemed suddenly very important. I had the singular mindset and the blissful oblivion of a tipsy grandparent. I was a menace. David looked frazzled when he found me in the bathroom, pill in hand. I was thinking, *All I need is a water glass for this pill. Shall we reassemble the shards on the steps?* Meanwhile, he was telling me the craziest thing I'd ever heard in my whole life.

"I don't think we'll be able to get a shirt on you," he said, "with the injury and the dish towel. We need to just go like this."

I dropped the pill into the sink. "I have to wear a shirt!" I cried, outraged.

"You can't handle a shirt!" he responded, very Jack Nicholson in *A Few Good Men*.

"*I don't care!*" I replied, like Tommy Lee Jones in *The Fugitive*.

We started to shout-enunciate nineties-film catchphrases at each other. I held fast, standing in the dark hallway by the front door, rapidly losing all the blood in my body. "I'm not going out in public wearing bloody sweat shorts and no shirt, David. I don't have my summer bod yet. I don't actually work out at the gym! I'm just there to make friends!" He seemed to understand that his beloved husband had lost his mind and patiently went to the closet and pulled out a bathrobe.

"We can drape this over you."

I recoiled. "Who am I, James Brown? I can't pull off that look. Just get me a hoodie. There's one in the second drawer in the closet. No, the second drawer. It's the purple one. It will match the shorts." There's one part of my brain that thought, *I'm being very clear about which hoodie I want.* And there's another part of my brain that thought, *You will die because of your vanity.* The two parts literally never meet.

All David wanted was to get his deranged husband some medical care. Meanwhile, I was having a fantastic time, hanging out with my arm above my head, debating clothing options like I was Joan Rivers on the red carpet. I had no worries whatsoever and was eager to start my Saturday errands. I have rarely been so relaxed in all my life. All it took was exsanguination.

David persuaded me to just throw the sweatshirt over my good arm like a shoulder fascinator. He went to put his shoes on, and suddenly I realized that a tank top would be perfect for this situation. So I wandered off again, this time into our study closet to look for the box the tank tops were in. How was I going to unpack this box while using one arm to hold a dish towel to another arm? Unclear. David, exasperated, found me with my head in a box, holding a vase that the movers, in their infinite wisdom, had thrown on top of the clothes.

"We have to find my tank tops," I said. I had the presence of mind to turn to him and confess, "I know I'm being ridiculous." Then I dove back into the box. I was going to have to pull all the tank tops out, because only one fit me at that point. I hoped David was excited for a fashion show!

I do fear that this is what I'm going to be like when I'm older. I want to be sitting in the park, talking about the soup I made to honor Audra McDonald's birthday. But it's possible that the chaotic energy I was throwing out is more my destiny. That's fine, too. For me at least. I was still really enjoying my own company. Maybe we don't have to choose between happiness and chaos. Steven Cole and Mrs. Peacock. Maybe I could have it all! (Well, I could have it all except for most of the blood in my body.)

David managed to get me out of the house sans tank top. Having made progress toward medical care, I began to feel very scared about the severity of my injury, which was an odd feeling because my utter amusement at the whole thing hadn't abated. If this is what crossing over to the other side is like, sign me up. Of course, we ran into the cool neighbors in the elevator. My hand was already raised above my head, so I proceeded to wave.

"Good morning!" I said to the neighbors. "I apologize for my exposed nipples."

They asked if I was going to be okay. Our longest conversation! David said yes. I said, "Who knows! Would you like to come to dinner tonight?"

———

We breezed into the empty waiting room of the closest urgent care. Everyone at urgent care seemed shocked at the sight of me, a person who needed urgent care. I was, at this point, like Gone Girl when she came back from Neil Patrick Harris's house. I had no shirt on, I looked like a Jackson Pollock painting, and I had a hoodie slung over one shoulder like a poorly styled early-2000s *Teen Beat* photo shoot.

"Good morning!" I called. "Do you do stitches? Just need a few, lol!" I was striding around like I'd thrown a party and invited everyone I knew. The medical assistant behind the triage desk looked stricken; his eyes bugged out of his head like we were robbing the joint. What were these people expecting to walk through the door if not medical problems of an urgent nature? They should have called the place Casual Care. Just Hanging Out Care. Pop In If You Need a Lozenge!

The assistant jumped up and led us back to some rooms. A doctor followed and started to take the dish towel off. David warned him that the wound was going to make a mess. The doctor ignored David. The room filled with blood like in *The Shining*. The doctor screamed. I giggled a little. Incredible! I thought churlishly, *Doctorman, honey, David told you what was going to happen, and look at you now. Have to change your lab coat.*

The doctor told us, "You gotta get out of here. You cut an artery." I didn't understand where he wanted us to go. The organic market next door? Fortunately, David was able to communicate like a human being and he asked the doctor where we should go if they couldn't help us. Meanwhile, I focused on the tongue depressors and remembered once accompanying a friend to the hospital when I was in my twenties. My friend stole all the tongue depressors when we left.

"I wonder why he did that," I said aloud to no one.

David and the doctor had a small back-and-forth about what hospital to go to, because we didn't know where the closest one was and apparently the doctor was not allowed to recommend one. I told him, "Look, if I survive this, I won't report you. My lips are sealed. I might write about this in a book. Who can say? Is there such a thing as a tongue encourager? I've been a little down in the mouth lately."

David shout-enunciated at him until he told us where to go in a general yet vague sense. He gave us directions in pig Latin. He was like, "Don't not go to Union Memorial." *Wink.* I applauded with my one good hand, because I simply adore farce.

We pulled up outside the hospital, and David jumped out to feed the parking meter. While he was gone, I seized the opportunity to try to wrestle my other arm into my hoodie for the sake of decorum. It was possible I was getting even more chaotic. I had stopped being a wacky eccentric and become an actual obstacle. My arm got stuck—*like he said it would*—so then I had to extricate myself before he came back and caught me. I was laughing and panicking at the same time and, honestly, I don't know why he married me. If you can believe it, I still had more blood left. I baptized the inside of my car and got out.

We went inside the ER and encountered a charge nurse who had the no-nonsense demeanor of someone Loretta Devine would play in a guest-starring role. I was immediately on board, because I love character actors. We gave our names, and she asked what we were there for. I replied, "I am covered head to toe with blood, alas." She asked how David was related and I got tense, slipping out of my delighted haze long enough to remember that simple facts about your life can become problems or points of attack. She'd asked a question and suddenly I remembered that we could be in danger, no matter what the law said. I could tell David sensed it, too.

"I'm his husband, we're married," he said confidently. The charge nurse wrote it down without comment.

They took me back to triage, and David tried to follow because he wanted to make sure that I was getting the right amount of care and he knew that I was not connected to reality. I needed his help. But this charge nurse was not interested in that one bit. David went to follow me through the door, and she bodily blocked him from entering the triage area. She told him, "Just sit down out there; you can come when he's taken to a room."

I got it, I know David got it, but in that moment I also knew that that was not going to sit right with him. It wasn't that he had a sense of entitlement so much as he felt a deep obligation to make sure things went smoothly for me. Which I thought was very sweet, as I watched the door close on him. With my arm still held aloft, I waved like I was sailing away on the *Titanic* and then asked another nurse where he got his cool earring.

I could see beyond the charge nurse into the waiting room, and I'd known David long enough to know that he wasn't simply going to accept getting turned away. Through the little triage window, I watched him march over to the waiting room area, and then David, love of my life, mild-mannered pastor, took a chair from the waiting room, scooted it in front of the triage window, and turned it around so he could face the charge nurse. And he waited.

Call him TNT, because he knows drama!

The charge nurse began, at full volume, talking about him. "Who he think he is?!" she asked the world. "He turned his chair around like he's in class." She continued like this for the entirety of my visit. What a couple of characters!

Eventually, they let David join me in a patient room. I told myself that after the excitement of the morning, I would need to calmly talk him down.

"Can you believe that doctor at urgent care didn't listen to you? What a lunatic!" I cried when he walked in.

"I know! Now he has to change his lab coat!" he shouted back.

And we shout-enunciated at each other like that for a while, as I got stitches, which is also disgusting.

The tension of the day melted away as we laughed about the charge nurse and the absurdity of the whole accident and the fact that we had to return to our half-unpacked apartment that now looked like a crime scene where Dr. Richard Kimble had been framed.

He asked about my pain level. I said it hurt but it was fine. He asked me if I was sure. I came out of my happy haze enough to wonder why he was pressing this question so much. He explained that the whole kerfuffle at the triage desk was because he was afraid I wasn't in the best position to advocate for myself. He said he knew that Black patients typically have their pain under-assessed in hospitals and he wanted to look out for me. I thought about how strange and perilous life can be if you go it alone. I thought, *How wonderful to have someone who wants to keep me alive. And, as much as any of us can be, free from pain.* My arm swaddled, we made our way out of the hospital, past the charge nurse, who was *still* talking about us.

"It's always difficult," I called, again summoning my best Mrs. Peacock, "when a group of new friends meet together for the first time, to get acquainted."

"What?" David asked.

"Nothing. Such a splendid day, right?!"

The Greatest City in America

When I was growing up, all the bus-stop benches in Baltimore had the same slogan painted on them: "Baltimore: the city that reads." It was meant to inspire literacy, which, at that point, the city was struggling with. Some figures put nearly a third of Baltimore's population as functionally illiterate in the late 1980s. So there was an aspirational quality as well to the bench slogan. It was like the Secret. (Though at this time the book about the Secret wasn't out yet. The Secret was still secret.) I don't know if benches were generally where people took their life-coaching advice from in those days, but I guess you have to start somewhere. A lot of people mocked the slogan. I heard "the city that bleeds" far more often than the original. I think this is the ongoing problem with Baltimore—no matter how many times the city presents itself as something new, there's always a counternarrative and a chorus of voices that say, "Nah, hon, I knew you when." As if a city can't be more than one thing. As if it isn't always changing. As if it isn't alive, even in the midst of so much death.

I always felt I *was* in the city that reads. My whole life in Baltimore was reading. My parents would take us to the library every week as kids, and I'd borrow the maximum number of items allowed, because it's not hoarding if it's books. As I grew older, I'd spend hours browsing the shelves and holed up in a corner, escaping to new worlds. After I came back from college, I took to going to the main branch of the city's free public library system, a breathtaking stone building that occupies an entire city block and features huge department-store-like windows at street level, which are famous for their book-themed displays. The central branch faces the Baltimore Basilica across the street and matches that building in grandeur and, to me, holiness.

Years later, the city seemed to right-size its self-perception by changing the slogan from "the city that reads" to simply "Believe." Baltimore is the original Ted Lasso; anyone who is still holding a grudge about the Colts will tell you, "Football is life." The mayor at the time, Martin O'Malley, described the campaign to *The New York Times* as "spiritual warfare," which takes a level of gumption that I can't help but respect. They painted "Believe" on the benches but also, incredibly, the city introduced a program to give out large black trash cans with the word "BELIEVE" painted in white on them. People went wild for this; who doesn't want a free trash can? As far as spiritual warfare goes, I think it was a good effort, but, I'm sorry, trash cans are an objectively hilarious space to put an encouraging message about a city's prospects. What was this brainstorming meeting like?

"How can we best capture the essence of the city?"

"Oh! I know. A receptacle for garbage but full of hope!"

Honestly, I've never identified with the city more.

"Believe," like "the city that reads," was an uncomfortable mix of inspirational and aspirational, but there was something poignant about the way the new slogan seemed at once a command and a plea. This campaign began in 2002, which was also the year I dropped out of college and moved back in with my parents. While I was residing at home, I was living in a state of depression, so the switch in the slogans also felt like a melancholy message specifically for my circumstance.

At that time, belief wasn't necessarily enough for me, but it was a start. Belief led to a change in the way I thought about what was possible in my life; thoughts led to actions; actions led to moving away again. I believed myself right out of Baltimore. But now I was back. And I couldn't find a trash can to save my life. And I was finding it hard to believe.

Baltimore was always reinventing itself, creating a new narrative from the beauty and the mess of the old. I wanted that, too, for myself. If only it was as easy as a coat of paint on a bench.

As David made his way through his first year as a solo pastor, his story became new in ways that were spectacular to me. He'd been brought in to help a small church's aging congregation and dwindling membership find new footing, and his energy and creativity for it seemed limitless. Over long days he was doing everything from meeting with current and former members to starting new programs to poring over the budget with the church's treasurer, figuring out how to make everything work. His sermons were vulnerable and witty and wise; he was intentional about sharing as much of himself as he could so that the congregation would feel empowered to share themselves with him. He spent weekends strategizing with other faith leaders in the area, planning with the caretakers of the church's apiary and memorial garden, and rearranging the way that the sanctuary was laid out to better accommodate the children and families that they hoped to soon welcome.

David was often the youngest person in the building on a Sunday. Far from being moribund or stuck in their ways, however, the congregation was alive and hungry for more life. The obstacles David faced that first year weren't resistance to change so much as fear that change wouldn't happen fast enough to keep the church afloat.

They were not afraid of making something new. They knew that creation, like faith itself, could be perilous, could evanesce in the absence of care. But they believed that the only way to survive was to keep creating.

In this generative space, my husband revealed a new version of himself. He was a maker, a co-creator. He believed, but more than belief—he acted.

Seeing him like this, so aligned with his purpose, I couldn't help but ask myself, *What am I making?*

I didn't attend the church very much. I would tell people that it was kind of like if your husband was a banker—you wouldn't go to the bank to watch them count money all day. And that was kind of true. There was a sense I couldn't shake that I was at my husband's job rather than in a place of spiritual transformation. And that made me feel like I was on the outside of yet another church in my life, despite how welcoming David's congregation was. But I was also unsure of whom I was supposed to be in the space. They'd had a first husband before—a man who was married to a previous pastor, a woman. He was still a member: a tall, genial older gentleman who was active on committees and took great pride in caring for the church's grounds. Yard work is not my ministry, so I decided I would keep the lawnmower in my prayers but maybe find some other way of being involved.

But what? The members of the church didn't seem to want anything more than my presence; David told me he was fine with whatever level of participation I felt comfortable with.

But, as with so many other aspects of life in Baltimore, I felt like I wasn't doing something right. Maybe this was something that one talked about with their pastor; I was sure David fielded queries about life's unanswered questions from his congregation all the time. I considered putting on a disguise and moseying up to the church grounds to start a therapeutic caper, but it seemed easier to just use the insurance that I got through David to find someone else to talk to. My Baltimore therapist was a friendly, mild-mannered guy named Brian who was about my age and had a slight Southern accent that would peek out on certain words. He was a reader, too, and we would sometimes talk about books, which was delightful. One of his favorite authors, and mine, was Ann Patchett, so if things ever got too intense in my work on myself, I would just bring up a plot point in *Bel Canto* to try to deflect.

At the beginning, I explained to him, "Nothing is wrong, but I can't really get started here, and I feel like I've lost the bead on my life. Also, I'm in a toxic relationship with the city of Baltimore, and so I guess I'm seeking couples counseling."

"For you and your husband?" he asked.

"No, for me and the city."

I told him that the years I'd spent in therapy in Philly had really helped to clarify some of the obstacles I encountered in childhood and my college years. "So I don't have any issues to work out with my past," I said foreshadowingly. "I just need to fix the present."

I explained that I was in an exciting but sometimes perplexing place in my life. "I'm struggling to make real-life connections, but I'm well-known online. I have tens of thousands of Twitter followers. Shouldn't that make me happy?" He was very good at talking me through the specifics of my rapidly changing career, but he promised, out of professional decorum, to never google me or read anything I published, which is the rudest damn thing I have ever heard in my life.

I told him that I felt this pressure to be content with our new lives, because David seemed so content, and things were going well for both of us, jobwise. When I sold my first book, I told him that I was excited and nervous but also that I felt a strange emptiness. "This is what I wanted. Shouldn't it feel different?"

"How do you want to feel?" Brian asked.

"I have no idea. Can we call Ann Patchett and see what she has to say about this?"

It felt silly to have problems. Things were fine. There were even great days. "This should be the best day of my life!" I exclaimed in therapy when news broke of my book. "Why is it giving me so much anxiety?"

We're all, I think, in pursuit of a good day. But having the best day of your life? That's a lot of pressure.

Brian suggested that these were normal concerns to have as one approached middle age.

I said, "Approach middle age?! Excuse me while I launch myself into the sun." At the time I was thirty-seven, although I didn't look a day over twenty and anyone who says otherwise is a liar. I don't have any interest in conceiving of my own mortality, but I guessed mathematically it was possible that I was getting somewhere close to the neighborhood of the Middle. I would concede that. But the prospect of beginning a midlife crisis was giving me a midlife crisis. "To paraphrase Danny Glover in *Lethal Weapon*, I'm too young for this shit!" I declared as I slathered hyaluronic acid on my face.

But—okay, brace yourself—I have bad news. In the *Lethal Weapon* movies, Danny Glover plays a perpetually exhausted middle-aged cop who famously and repeatedly declares, "I'm getting too old for this shit." Did you know he was only forty the first time he said it onscreen? Welcome to my spiral.

"Do you want to talk about why thinking about Danny Glover and your best days has you spiraling?" Brian asked.

I pulled out a copy of *The Dutch House* by Ann Patchett and read for the rest of our session.

Many people claim that their wedding was the best day of their lives. I find this fascinating. I had a wonderful time at my wedding and our friends still talk about it, usually when David and I bring it up by asking, "Would everyone like to go around and say nice things about our wedding? We can't serve dessert until everyone participates!" The album that I made from the wedding photos should win some sort of award from Shutterfly, and I will keep tweeting them about it until they relent.

But was it the best day of my life? I'm not so sure, no offense. No offense to David. No offense to Shutterfly (please check your DMs). No offense to me, myself, the other person who got married.

My wedding was a lovely affair and also a lot of work and also, as my days tend to be, extremely anxiety-producing. I was getting married in front of God and everyone. I cried in public like I'd won an Oscar. I kept worrying that an ex was going to burst through the door and make a scene, even though all of my exes are like, "Yeah, I think we're good here, but Godspeed!" I had a great time that I barely remember. I didn't even have the presence of mind to eat dessert! A breach of my personal code of conduct! Sorry, but skipping dessert is an immediate disqualification in my book. This day can't even crack the top 10.

And even though that felt reasonable to say in therapy, it still made me sad. But then again, isn't the idea of marriage that you're launching yourselves into a whole new spectrum of days?

For better or worse, in boom times and bust, in going viral and in getting canceled, in "our kid got into college" and in "our kid got into college and we have to pay for it." In the unimaginable and, well, the unimaginable. There's a part of me that believes that getting married is saying, "I don't know what the best day is going to be, but I can't wait to find out with you." It's also saying, "I'm excited to take turns taking out the garbage for the rest of our lives," but let's be a little more romantic here. Let's be a little more expansive. Let's take the ceiling off this house and look at the sky. Getting married, in some small way, is a mutual agreement to hope—to hope it will work out until it doesn't, to hope it won't hurt too much until it does, to hope that being together is better than being apart, to hope that something beautiful and sustaining will flourish. To make something out of the beauty and the mess. And part of that hope is the belief that the best is waiting out there for us just beyond today's horizon.

By the time we moved back to Baltimore, the "Believe" trash cans were long gone and the benches had yet another slogan painted on them. This city has had more eras than Taylor Swift. The slogan that greeted us as we arrived was "Baltimore: the greatest city in America." And at that point I was like, "Okay, absolutely not." Babe. This feels like shade. The *greatest* city? In America?? Better than Chicago? Better than Pawnee, Indiana?! Better than the murder capital of the world, Cabot Cove, Maine? Okay . . .

I refused to engage with it. I was like, "This bench is going through a midlife crisis. I will respectfully avert my gaze."

If this city couldn't figure out what it wanted to be, I decided, then there was no way that I was going to figure out my relationship to it. And if this *was* the greatest city and these were potentially the best days, why didn't I feel it? Why was I the only person, even in my own house, who wasn't feeling it?

Brian suggested that my old middle-aged ass should look into mindfulness. "It might help you to focus only on the present for a little while. Not worrying about the past or the future. Just be aware of where you are."

"I'm aware of where I am," I quipped. "That's the problem."

He continued, "Ask yourself, where am I now? I'm in a chair. I'm in an office. What am I feeling now? Hunger, contentment, annoyance, what have you. Just keep asking yourself. Where am I now? How do I feel now? Where am I now?"

As we neared a year in Baltimore, at the end of 2018, I suggested to David that we should become the kind of people who send out holiday letters. It felt like a good way to reach out to those we felt distant from, to remind ourselves that what our lives had been wasn't gone. I downloaded the addresses from our wedding thank-you notes, and we decided we would take turns working in a Google Doc to create the letter.

David went first. A day or two later, he told me that his half was done, and I could write mine. I opened the document and there were five single-spaced pages of text already there. I thought it was incredible and hilarious. I told him, "Babe! What is this? No one wants to read all that about someone else's life! Now, if you'll excuse me, I have to return to writing my three-hundred-page memoir."

What he wrote, however, was wonderful. Funny and vulnerable and open and honest. He had this hilarious bit about fonts up top—comedy queen!—and then he seamlessly launched into a record of what had been a hard but inspiring year. He

wrote about his work at the church and an award he'd received
from his college. He wrote of our joy about our new niece and
the pain he felt watching his father and his uncle navigate cancer treatments. He wrote about how isolated he'd felt, too, in
our apartment at the bottom of the hill. He wrote, in a section
he titled "Setbacks," about missing friends, about his own
struggles with anxiety, about loneliness.

His openness made me feel closer to him, but it also made
me sad. We were in this together, but there were still things we
had to do on our own.

He ended it talking about hope. Trips we were going to take,
new levels of career achievement he was hoping to reach. The
best, getting nearer and nearer.

I stared at the document on and off for days. I didn't want to
edit it down; the fullness of his experience was beautiful to me.
But I didn't want to write anything of what I'd experienced in it.
I didn't want to tell the story I was living. I felt ashamed. I was
waiting on the new coat of paint. So I let the letter go. I said we
shouldn't send one at all. Think of the postage and the printing!

But I wished, even as I archived the document, that I hadn't
pooh-poohed the idea. I wished I'd embraced the opportunity
and written five of my own pages to accompany his. I wished
I'd been able to be vulnerable and introspective and hopeful
and honest. I wished we'd paid for extra postage and those
large manila envelopes to ship the stack of paper. I wished we'd
bought those adorable tiny binder clips to keep it all together. I
wished I'd taken the chance to let our friends, our loved ones,
those we care about, know how we were and where we were
going.

I wished I'd let myself ask the question that I was so fearful
of: Who am I now? Who am I now? Who am I now? Who am I
now?

You Said You Outside, But You Ain't That Outside

There are a lot of events in my life that I think back on and wonder how things would have been different had I chosen another path. Mostly those events are meals where I didn't order the special. But, I suppose, I consider bigger things, too. I tease out the series of events in the alternative reality until I reach a point where I find myself more unhappy than I am now. Then I end the simulation, satisfied with my choices. I am obsessed with doing this. I think it's because I grew up on a steady diet of evangelical Christianity and Nora Ephron movies, both of which prize consequence and near misses and the magical reward of a happily ever after to those who are worthy and choose right.

This isn't to say I make the right choices in life all the time. Or even most of the time. I'm constantly making absolutely terrible life choices and paying the price! I am a cautionary tale. But there's a certain comfort, I think, in reviewing some other version of my life and going, "Hmmph, this story sucks! Give me my old problems, please!"

The one choice I never play this game with, however, is the decision to get engaged. And maybe that sounds cutesy or overly confident, like one of those twee couples who have a home-renovation show on cable and then get messily divorced years later but still must finish their contract with the network.

I don't mean it like that. I simply mean that when the decision presented itself, it didn't feel like a forked path; it felt like a bend in the road toward the future. It felt different. A doorway opened that said, "This is your life," and I walked through.

I write all of this and yet the fact remains that the week David and I went on our first date, I actually had two dates scheduled. (Yes, that's right: I am hot.) David and I were to get dinner on a Tuesday, and another guy and I were to get brunch the Sunday prior. Both of these dates had sprung from a one-man show I was performing called *Always the Bridesmaid*, which was seventy-five minutes of me talking about how much I would like to go on a date. Unsuccessful in dating throughout my twenties, I'd devoted my thirties to being unsuccessful theatrically. David and the other guy were both in attendance at the show, which is all the encouragement I needed. I was looking for a spouse, but mostly I was looking for someone who would pay an admission fee for my nonsense.

The brunch date was nice, but at the end of it he said he had work to do to get ready for the week and I said I had work to do to get ready for the week and we parted ways. And every once in a while, I wonder what would have happened if we'd just decided to do our work for the week together instead of what actually happened, which was splitting up and then running into each other later at a coffee shop with our laptops. If I were writing this as a movie, the coffee shop is where the spark would have happened. But it didn't, and I think that's conclusive evidence.

Two days later, David and I went to dinner and talked for four hours, then went on three more dates in the next week, and a few months later casually started talking about what it might be like to get engaged. We had both been thinking about it for a while, perhaps the whole time, perhaps from the moment the lights went up on my one-man show. (Well, probably not then, but one really shouldn't discount the power of live theater.) I had always imagined I'd get engaged at the trendy sushi restaurant that I'd been fired from five years earlier. I started daydreaming about it while I was still working there—it would be cute; the ring would be placed on top of one of the maki coming around the rotating sushi conveyor belt! I simply didn't see why me getting the boot in an embarrassing fashion should interrupt my plans for romantic nonsense. Hadn't I suffered enough?

David had a slightly different idea. He's always wanted to get engaged on a hike. I was like, "Okay, but who will make the maki?" I was fine with a hike, I supposed, but I'd really hoped for my happiest moment in life to occur in front of a restaurant general manager who had once handed me a severance letter and COBRA information while a Godzilla movie played on a big-screen TV over his shoulder. The conversation about maybe possibly getting engaged turned into a conversation about maybe possibly going on a hike, which turned into a conversation about maybe possibly going on a trip to one of David's favorite hiking spots in Oregon to get engaged. One thing led to another, like dots on a map, because in some ways we always just knew. As Nora Ephron would say, like you know about a good melon.

But the thing is, this trip we were talking about? The one where we'd exchange engagement rings and change our Facebook statuses? The thing I was so sure about? David wanted the event to occur at the top of a mountain. One that we walked up with our feet and bodies and such. This was a problem. I've never climbed to a mountaintop. Who am I, Dr. Martin Luther King, Jr.? But to David, who is more well traveled than me and has been to more marches, this was old hat.

To say David is outdoorsy is an understatement. He's an Eagle Scout, for one, which is basically like having a graduate degree in being outside. He told me early in our relationship about a great trip he took ice-caving. As in sleeping in a cave of ice like he was Superman retreating to the Fortress of Solitude. I was under the impression that's only something you did out of necessity if you got caught in an avalanche on Everest. And I knew that's a situation in which I'd never find myself, because I firmly believe that Mount Everest is none of my business. David likes walking in nature and planting stuff and having dirt from the ground under his nails after a hard day's labor. He lived for a summer in Japan, biking back and forth to a rice paddy where he . . . harvested rice, I guess. I still don't know, actually. We've talked about it a lot, and every time I nod and smile, but he might as well be describing a jaunt to Saturn. How is rice grown? On a tree? I don't know; it's none of my business!

I knew this about him going in, and it was dawning on me that being in a long-term relationship with someone meant getting to know the places where you differ and sometimes moving closer together and sometimes walking parallel paths, preferably one of those paths being indoors at an air-conditioned mall. But I didn't realize that I'd have to deal with it so soon. I wondered, for the first time, *Do we want different things?*

But for David, I agreed to go outside. There was a place in his home state of Oregon that had been special to him for a long time, and he'd always imagined hiking up it and getting engaged just as the sun slipped below the horizon. It was called Black Butte, which I thought was hilarious until he informed me it's pronounced "beaut." He thought we should fly out there, do the hike, exchange engagement rings, and then spend a few days in a funky nearby hotel called McMenamins, which had been built inside a repurposed school. He showed me pictures of the hotel pool with a hole cut in the ceiling to let in the night air and a glimpse of the stars. He pointed out a movie theater on the property in an old auditorium full of couches and the speakeasy in the broom closet. He was appealing to my love of hotels, my inherent desire for aesthetically pleasing nonsense, and my affinity for cocktails made by hipsters with handlebar mustaches. He knew how to get me to the mountain.

As we planned, I'd repeatedly make my very hilarious MLK mountaintop joke. And every time David would remind me that Black Butte was actually a stratovolcano. Then I'd reply, "A what?! Dr. Martin Luther King, Jr., did not fight for civil rights so I could be going up some damn subclass of geological formation. We gotta go to Everest! Do it for Bayard Rustin!"

We flew to Oregon in the middle of the summer and stayed with David's mom for a few days before driving out to the city of Three Sisters, so named because of a string of three closely spaced *actual* mountains. I got very excited about this, because for most of my twenties I had attempted to write a misbegotten modern adaptation of Anton Chekhov's play *Three Sisters*, set at a beach house and focusing on three gay best friends who want to go to Manhattan. "I'm a huge Chekhov fan," I told David as we drove into town. "Let me guess, the mountains are named Olga, Masha, and Irina?"

"Actually," he replied, "they're named Faith, Hope, and Charity."

I pulled the emergency brake and got out of the car. Can you believe this?! Who the hell are they?

———

Before we went to Black Butte, we stopped by REI, where David of course has a membership. I had never been inside an REI before, and I found it delightful because I didn't understand the practical function of a single thing in the store. David got busy stocking up on supplies we'd need. He got little packets that warmed your hands when you cracked some goo inside them; he got jerky for us to snack on; he got us headlamps and flashlights; he bought me some cargo pants that unzip at the knee to become shorts, because it was going to be hot going up and cold going down but apparently 1997 the whole time. He picked up one of those silver Mylar blankets they give you when you've finished a marathon. "What's that for?" I asked. He explained that if I fell off the side, I should wrap myself in it to keep warm and to catch the attention of the rescue helicopter.

I said, "If I do what now?"

I was, unfortunately, of no use on this shopping excursion, so I did the thing that everyone loves when trying to stock up on lifesaving materials: small comedy bits. I took a picture of a mannequin in some kind of wearable sleeping bag and posted it on Facebook with the caption "Found my outfit for prom." I grabbed a machete and jokingly asked David if we should buy it.

"It might be helpful," he said seriously, "for the bobcats."

"For the bob-who now?" I asked, but he was already heading to the checkout counter.

We loaded our REI purchases into the rental car and continued on to the hike. In the bathroom of a rest stop, we assembled two backpacks and I changed into some ugly clothes with good heating and cooling properties. And up we went. David had done the hike many times in his life; it marked meaningful moments, and he was eager to share it. And I, despite all my protestations, was eager to experience it with him. A nice thirty-minute walk up a mountain sounded perfect to me.

What I had neglected to ask, I realized about fifteen minutes in, was how long this whole thing was going to take. David was a little anxious because he wanted us to get to the top just before sunset; he had a whole plan. Sunset wasn't for another hour and a half, so I didn't get what the big deal was. He informed me that it was two miles to the top and it would take us probably two hours. "Of continuous forward momentum?" I cried. I tried to convince him that it was not too late to go to a Benihana.

But we were already partway up, and we'd told all of our friends we'd post a video with the view in the background, and REI doesn't sell green screens, so we had little choice but to reach the top before sunset. And I kept stopping to take pictures because it was quite beautiful and I wanted to remember it and, against my very nature, I had started to enjoy, well, nature. I could tell all my lollygagging was starting to stress David out. He told me we could take photos of the scenery on the way down, but I was 75 percent sure I was going to fall off the side and have to be rescued by helicopter and/or bobcat, so I really wanted to get it all on the first take.

Finally, we reached the top, just as the sun was nearing the horizon. And it was as beautiful as David had described it, offering a 360-degree view of the surrounding land, with Masha, Olga, and Irina visible nearby and, through the haze, Mount Hood in the distance. There were a couple of other hikers milling about, but it mostly felt like we had the entire stratovolcano to ourselves. I was stunned by David's ability to create a dramatic moment with something as unruly as nature. What had started as a casual low-stakes conversation about spending the rest of our lives together had ended up here, on top of the world. It seemed unlikely, improbable, but there'd only been one path up.

David suggested we make a cairn, which is a pile of rocks

that hikers will use to mark a place in their journey, so that they know where they've been and can find their way back. David mentioned that in mountaineering, cairns also mark places where it's difficult to determine which way to go; they mark struggle and decision-making. And, he told me, for the ancient Hebrew people traveling through the wilderness, cairns were used to signify places where they'd encountered God. This pile of rocks could be all of those things for us. He said that the cairn would always mark this place in our journey and the covenants we made, and when we came back it would remind us that we were here and that our path from this point would be different.

He pulled out the rings we'd ordered online and some promises he'd written for us to say to each other. I think maybe I was supposed to also write something, but I was like, "You know I'm no good with words."

And it's just as well, because as soon as I started reading aloud what he'd written, while the sun touched down on the horizon, I became overwhelmed by the realization that this person loved *me*. The long, strange, frustrating, lonely, sometimes sad path of my life had led me up this peak, past this pile of rocks, and to this person, who had crossed the country to find me and then crossed back with me to make a commitment. And I realized that I hadn't believed it was possible before this moment. As much as I let my thinking get magical and as much as I rewatched Nora Ephron movies and as much as I went on brunch dates and wrote solo shows with the sole purpose of getting said brunch dates, I just didn't believe, deep inside, that someone was waiting for me down the path. I didn't believe I deserved it. I didn't think I was in the right story. I had wanted it so bad, but I had learned by this point that wanting something in this world won't bring it any closer.

And yet here I was, miles above the world, closer than ever.

I don't think I ever really considered what vows were until this moment, even though we weren't reciting vows, even though this wasn't a marriage. I never really thought about the weight of a promise to love. How you can't possibly articulate what you're committing to and yet how your heart and another person's heart just know. They know in a way that transcends time and space and anything that has gone before. It's an act so all-encompassing that the only place to do it is on the top of the mountain, at the edge of the sky.

I started to cry. I'm not a crier, so this was surprising to me. I started to cry so hard that I was shaking. And then I got embarrassed that the other hikers were going to think David was breaking up with me. This was really what I was worried about in this moment.

I pulled myself together enough to take some photos and then we watched the sun slip below the horizon, and almost immediately as it did, I felt all the adrenaline leave my system and I started to violently shiver. I'd gone from being sweaty and hot in my convertible shorts, hysterically crying, to struggling to zip on the bottoms of my pants and cracking the hand warmers that David had purchased. I was extremely confused. I was like, "David, I think nature is trying to kill me!"

I couldn't stop shaking. I was so cold. We decided I needed to get off the mountain and into the car. "Great," I said. "That'll be about thirty minutes, right?"

Darkness fell quickly and the temperature went with it. We descended from the peak and into the tree line. My fingers were going numb, which scared me. I had just gotten this ring and now I was about to lose the whole damn finger? Dr. Martin

Luther King, Jr., would never stand for that. I told David about my hands, and his Eagle Scout training kicked in. He told me we had to hurry down to get me warmed up. So then we were literally running down the side of a volcano, like extras in a movie featuring Dwayne Johnson. "See," I said, my teeth chattering, "this is why I took pictures on the way up. So you'll have something to remember me by."

No matter how fast we hustled, however, the distance was what it was, and the terrain was what it was, and that meant we were still a couple of hours from our destination. Maybe that's a metaphor for marriage—moving together through the darkness, as fast as you can, knowing that the only way through is through. Maybe. I didn't know that then. And that's the point, right? Because if you know how hard it might be to get down from the mountain, you might not ever go up.

You Rock

"What happens in 'Cinderella'?" I asked a class full of high schoolers. I was at a Jewish day school where one of my best friends from high school, Lisa, was a teacher. One of her colleagues was doing a unit on storytelling, and Lisa had invited me to give a workshop for them. This was my first time doing this kind of work in my capacity as a full-time writer, and I was thrilled. I loved being introduced as someone who made money telling stories; I loved the way the teacher told the class to be impressed that I had a book coming out. Honestly, I love anyone who convinces a teenager to be impressed by me for any reason. And I loved running my story workshop.

I've been doing a version of this for years, even before my primary vocation was writing-related. I used to have business cards that read, "R. Eric Thomas—storyteller," and people would look at the cards and go, "Like . . . do you talk about *Anansi the Spider*?" And I'd go, "No, I just talk about my life." And they'd go, "That's therapy." And I'd go, "Never heard of it."

In the workshops, I usually like to start off by having the group plot out the action of a fairy tale together. This always goes chaotically. See, the issue is that I think of fairy tales as a common text with which we're all familiar. But I've learned when teaching adults that many don't really remember the details or never heard them to begin with. And when teaching kids, I discover that the versions of fairy tales that they know are informed by new cartoon movies that I've never seen. One time I asked a class to name the main characters in "Rapunzel" and someone called out, "The horse!" I was like, "What the hell are you talking about, young buck?" Apparently, this is a character from the Disney movie *Tangled*. Sorry, I missed it. I get all my fairy-tale knowledge from the PBS broadcast of the 1987 production of *Into the Woods,* as the Grimms intended.

I've found that "Cinderella" works best in these lessons. After we identify the characters, I ask what the main character wants. We then plot out the action of the story by asking if the main character is getting closer to or farther away from what she wants. What I like about "Cinderella" is that if we decide, as a group, that what she wants is a family—her mother has died, her father is absent, the stepfamily is mean—then she arrives at her happy ending the moment the fairy godmother appears. The rest—the prince, the shoe, the happily ever after—may be important, but a major part of her journey has already resolved. We know she's going to be okay.

The students at Lisa's school were engaged from the beginning, so bright, so invested, and so willing to jump into the next part of the workshop: telling their own stories. They were adept at framing and reframing their own experiences, talking about simple anecdotes featuring pets or parties and more-complex stories featuring loss and love. While they may not yet have experienced a lot of what life has to offer, they often homed in on stories from their grandparents and parents. In making those stories their own, the students relished questioning what they wanted and whether they got it and identifying the obstacles they overcame along the way. I adore this kind of work because it exposes me to new ways of thinking about narratives and puts new energy behind something I do every day.

Afterward, I hugged Lisa goodbye and thanked her for a great time. But the minute I walked out of the building, all the lightness dropped off me. Back to life. I climbed into my car and put my head on the steering wheel for thirty minutes, until I could muster the energy to go home. Even as I did it, I thought, *This is a very "movie character" thing to do. Do people in real life, when they're struggling emotionally, put their heads on steering wheels or run outside and scream or let a single tear slip past their eyelid? Fake!*

I kept having moments like that—I'd get energized by the work that I loved and then, when it was over, I'd be brought low by the prospect of the rest of my day. I loved my work, but my work was not saving me from the feeling that had become clearer and more pronounced over the year: a deep sense of hopelessness.

What did I want? To be happy. How did it end? I didn't know.

For most of my life I've gone through periods of depression, sometimes intense, sometimes more ambient. I'm tempted to say that I have a struggle with depression, because that's the commonly used phrase, but it's really more of an ongoing partnership than a struggle. Depression just hangs out with me like a lax babysitter who is ambivalent about my bedtime. Depression is a text conversation that ebbs and flows; every once in a while, Depression texts, "Have you seen this meme? It's going to psychologically wreck you for six months. Brunch soon?" Depression is like Jiminy Cricket riding around on my shoulder, but instead of acting as my conscience, it just mumbles, "You're bad, things are bad, and nothing will improve."

And at this point I'm just like, ". . . Okay." Like, we get it, girl. Thanks!

There were times in each decade of my life, sometimes spanning years, that it felt like an active crisis. It felt like there would be no end to it; it felt like I was my depression, like I was the one riding around on some person-shaped darkness shuffling through the world. But I've found that people tend not to react well when you say, "Oh, I'm just not feeling so well today because I'm Jiminy Cricketing an anthropomorphized darkness." So I don't talk about it, or I downplay it, or I say, "Well, what's to say?"

In Baltimore, on my less charitable days, I'd chastise myself for being depressed at all. *You have a job that pays you to write jokes and a husband you love and an apartment with a kitchen island. What do you have to be sad about?* I'd ask myself.

And then my brain would reply, *Damn, a dude can't even have a chemical imbalance without getting canceled? Wowwwww.*

Then I'd say, *You know that cancel culture isn't a real thing and it's irresponsible in this political climate to even joke about it. What you're talking about is consequence culture.*

I had started taking mental-health days to get away from the work of making comedy out of the bottomless pits of Trump news cycles, to give myself some new energy, and to connect to the hope. Taking a mental-health day when you work from home feels a little silly, though. You're emailing HR like, "For personal reasons, I will be staying in bed as usual."

It's always nice when a job just lets you take a day without a lot of explanation, because it's yours and you have every right to. Some jobs make you do a whole song and dance to justify the day. To get approved for a sick day, you have to perform the end of *La Bohème*. Those are usually the jobs that exacerbate the need to take the day. Emailing HR like, "As you are aware: Y'all make me sick!" I've had plenty of those jobs in the past.

At those bad jobs where I had to really elaborate on my need for a mental-health day, I'd stare at the blank request form like I was George R. R. Martin trying to finish the long-gestating final book of *Game of Thrones*. I'm a writer, and I don't want to turn in subpar work.

I'd start typing into the form: "As you know, I'm sad. What else . . . what else . . . ?" And then I'd start rattling off potential causes, like I was Cyrano de Bergerac listing insults. "Why am I sad, you ask? Well, I'm Black in America. I'm gay in America. I'm American in America. The ozone layer is fixed, but everything else? Not so great! I still haven't found a church that I really love. I miss it. I didn't eat today. Whoops! Sometimes I think about the opportunities that my ancestors didn't get, and it really devastates me. I'm worried that my 401(k) will not save me from being lonely as a senior. Hey, quick question: Is this all there is? I watched *The Hours* at a very pivotal moment in my development, and I think it changed me. Right now I'm at a Meryl-Streep-in-the-kitchen level. I'll let you know if we get to a full Nicole."

HR writes back: "Received."

None of the reasons were really *the* thing, but I don't think there is just one thing. Whatever the components of my depression, I've never wanted them to define me. I feel that the other parts of me—the part that gets up every day and finds genuine humor in odd places, the part that hungers for community, the part that always strains to reach the end of the story—these are the real parts. So sometimes when I have to acknowledge the dark part, to say that I'm really struggling and ask for help, I feel like I'm talking about the inner workings of a stranger. The sadness is real and it is always around and it is not who I am.

Fortunately, at *ELLE* they didn't make me jump through hoops to take my days. I just emailed my editor and she wrote back, "Of course! I hope everything is okay!" No matter how you describe it, no matter why you need it, I think you always want someone on the other side of the request who expresses a little bit of care.

On the first mental-health day, it felt like a good idea to get out of the house, so I went to the mall. Perhaps buying things would make me happy! Unfortunately, my understanding of Maryland geography is untethered from reality, and the mall I wanted to go to was an hour away from home. But I didn't have anything better to do, so I drove.

I sat at the mall for a while, just watching walkers in jogging clothes and parents with young kids and chaperones from adult daycare centers and a couple of teens skipping school pass by. Sometimes I'd see a young professional strolling through, and I'd think, *Why aren't they at work?* And then I'd think, *They're probably asking the same question about you.* And then I'd wonder, *Are we all just experiencing mental-health crises at the mall?*

I can tell something is going wrong for me when I withdraw—I stop caring as much about the things I usually care about, be it keeping up the house or maintaining social connections or even watching the shows I like. But the more insidious thing that happens is that I lose track of my story. I lose track of where I'm going. I stop wanting to go anywhere. I stop thinking about getting to my desired ending, because everything feels like an ending already.

Eventually, I decided that it was a little too much, even at this low emotional point, for me to just sit forlornly in the half-empty mall all day. And so that's when I decided to go to the cemetery.

In the moment, I really thought it was a logical next step in my day of depression errands. I remembered (incorrectly) that the cemetery where my maternal grandparents were buried was near the mall. I hadn't been as an adult. I had a car now. Why not go pay my respects?

Of course, the cemetery was actually forty minutes away from the mall. So then I thought, since I was going, I should also go to the place where my paternal grandparents were buried. All very normal errands. But a cemetery is not an errand. A cemetery is not Meryl Streep in *The Hours* shopping for an enormous bouquet of flowers. Ever present in these periods of depression are hazy existential questions: What is this all for? What are you working so hard for? What are you living for? Who do you care about? Who cares about you? And those questions become sharper when you consider that all of this will end.

Well, no, not all of it. Something remains. You don't go to the cemetery to visit the stone. You go to visit the memory. In continuum, there's hope.

Just before my parents entered their forties, my mother's father died of a heart attack. As the decade progressed, both of their mothers would grow sick and pass away. As I remembered it, my parents' forties had been grueling. And I talked with Brian in those early therapy sessions about the anxiety that that produced, sensing that my incoming forties were going to bring about a series of life changes I didn't want. My parents, during

their forties, went through difficult job transitions and sometimes struggled to make ends meet. My memory of them in
those years is mixed—they were present and giving and our
house was often full of joy, but the toll of the challenges they
faced in these middle years of life was evident.

They were hard years for them. Even though we still gathered around the table for meals, even though there were happy
times and they had professional successes and personal growth
and family vacations, I could sense the hardness. And I understood it with more dimension now as an adult, with my own
happy times and professional successes and vacations. Looking
back, I wish that I could have made it easier for my parents
somehow, which is a futile wish for a child. But I'm not a child
now.

That's the thing about memory—it never fully situates you
in the past. There's a part of me that is at the table with them,
or in front of the TV, or riding to school in the back of the car.
And there's a part of me that is in my own car in the present,
driving from the mall. Those parts can't reach each other. They
can only look.

I went first to the cemetery where my mother's parents are buried. Though they were Black, their graves are in a predominantly white burial ground, which was near the nursing home
where my grandmother moved after my grandfather died. As I
drove, I tried to call back their memories. It's easy, especially
after decades, to first remember the harder things—the injuries
and illness that were harbingers of what was to come. A fall at
a holiday dinner, a car accident, the series of strokes that pro-
gressively incapacitated my grandmother. When aphasia would
steal a word from her, she'd cry with force, "Oh, *heck*." But

before, further back, there's more. A jar filled with peanut M&M's on their sideboard. The smell of their house: cedar and his pipe tobacco. She was a reader. Curious, persistent. When she had to transfer up north to a predominantly white Philadelphia high school in her senior year and they refused to take her credits, she started over. She graduated anyway. He was the first person my mother called for advice, for help, for a kindness. The memory of him lumbering up the stairs in my house as my brothers and I cowered in fear of a mouse that had gotten stuck. The way he captured it effortlessly, devilishly dared us to look, and then turned and walked back down and out of the house, still holding the mouse. The cement yard behind their small rowhome; in the back, a garden in pots. My grandmother rattling off the names of plants. The aroma of honeysuckle. Walter and Clara.

I parked and made my way up a hill to the cemetery office to see if I could get help locating the grave. Inside, a lanky, bald white man with glasses swooped around the corner, expeditious, like a vampire party host. "Can I help you?" he whispered, though to me it sounded like "Hurp?" He had the kind of stoic expression you'd expect from someone working the office at a cemetery, but he still seemed surprised to see me.

I told him what I was there for. He nodded silently and motioned for me to follow as he glided into his office, slid a chair out for me, glided into his chair, glided through the log-in screen on the computer, and asked me my grandmother's name. It was so quiet in his office that I whispered my answer. I wondered what it was like to be so still all day long.

The grave was exactly where he said it would be, at the bend of one of the roads, near the crest of a hill. There was a bouquet of faded artificial flowers in the metal vase between my grandmother and grandfather's names. As I drove by to park, I noticed what looked like trash on the grave, as well. As I got closer, I saw that the trash was actually the ruin of two Mylar balloons tied to the vase. One had been ripped apart by the elements, and only the word "birthday" remained. I couldn't call to mind my grandfather's birthday in the moment but knew my grandmother's was near Thanksgiving. Had this been here since November? Could it have survived—such as it was—for nine months? I lifted the other balloon, still wet from the rainstorm the night before. It was intact though deflated. And it read, "You Rock!"

I gasped upon seeing it. If you had asked me what I thought the balloon might say, I would never have come up with "You Rock!" I would have lost that *Family Feud* round every single time. Now, what did it mean? I looked around as if I could figure out who had left it and for what reason by using nonexistent context. Here were the clues: I was in a graveyard; there were balloons. End of clues. I was at a loss.

I looked at it again. The word choice was so funny to me, though I tried to force myself to ignore that out of reverence. The phrase was casual, modern, I couldn't fathom a scenario in which it would apply to my grandmother, who died at ninety in the year 2000. Make no mistake, she did rock, but I doubted it would have occurred to me to go to a store and buy a balloon that said so. It had occurred to someone, though, which was delightful. Maybe it should have occurred to me, too. I hadn't brought anything, hadn't even thought to bring flowers. I had come to them empty-handed and blue, looking for hope in context, and I found a party.

I couldn't make sense of it, but I also didn't want to. This was someone else's offering. Trying to make sense of it would be intrusive, I thought. The same as if someone had driven up while I stood by the graveside and asked why I'd spent the morning sitting sadly in a mall and then visiting my grandparents' grave for the first time in nearly twenty years. The same as if they'd tried to ascribe meaning to it without knowing the whole story.

"You Rock!" the balloon said excitedly. Here, in the all-encompassing quietude of the cemetery: an exclamation point. The shock of life. I took another look and then carefully placed the balloons back where they were.

I knew that my paternal grandparents were in a Black cemetery, but I couldn't remember the name. It seemed likely that calling my parents and telling them, "I'm going through a *thing* so I'd like to go on a walking tour of family grave sites; can you give me the addresses?" might ring an alarm bell, so instead I sat in my car, paid for a subscription to a newspaper site, and looked up my own grandparents' obituaries. It was not a cry for help; it was research.

My father's father died before I was born. A preacher. A man with dozens of little jobs to make ends meet. A worker. A smiling round face in a sepia-toned photo of him in his late fifties, my grandmother's arms around his neck. That photo stayed on her wall the entire time she lived in the apartment on the first floor of our house. All of her photos were covered in Saran Wrap and thumbtacked to the walls. I'd visit daily and I'd stare at her in the photo. Dark-brown skin, white hair cut close in a natural, smile huge. Her voice was like a fire alarm, high-pitched and throaty at the same time. The sound of it charging up through the floors of our house, from her apartment underneath. Hymns. Other times she would let loose a scream in mock frustration that barely masked something truer, deeper. On car rides to appointments, we'd pass one particular stretch of road and every time it would remind her of her brother and prompt her to remark, "Uncle Steve sends his love." Her favorite treats: Cafe Vienna International Coffee in the tin can, which I thought was very fancy, and a little swirled pecan roll.

When I pulled up to the second cemetery, they were getting a delivery, and two grounds workers and two staff members, all Black, were standing in the vestibule, supervising. The staff members greeted me as I approached and ushered me into the lobby with a "Good afternoon, sir." Two Black receptionists sat behind a desk, mid-conversation. I told them I was looking for my grandparents and gave my grandmother's name.

"What year?"

"1995," I answered.

The other one was pleasantly surprised. "You had that right away! Most people are like, 'Well, lemme call Shirley, cuz she got her knee replaced that year so she'll know, or maybe I can ask Roscoe . . .'" The women laughed and so did I. It was the first time I'd laughed all day. The lobby smelled like coconut lime verbena, which reminded me of high school in a good way. The way that everybody hung out at the mall for fun and not just depression; the way we'd go slather on samples at Bath & Body Works. There was so much activity around me and, having been alone all day, I drank it in. Black people in business clothes milled about, officious-looking older folk, young office workers, all in clothes ironed to a crisp. White shirts and blouses, dark trousers, salt-and-pepper hair: Everything was monochrome but vibrant, alive and Black.

A woman standing by the door to the office called into the main reception area. One of the receptionists owed her some paperwork. The receptionist rolled around the corner and chirped, "I'm helping this gentleman now!" as she handed over a card. The woman from the office spotted me and smiled apologetically as the receptionist rolled back to her desk, chuckling.

They found the site and drew me a map. Someone came over to collect money for the lottery buy-in from the receptionists. A nattily dressed older Black man walked out of the office, the coat of his sharp brown suit slung over his arm. He greeted me warmly: "They taking care of you all right, sir?" I said they were, and he nodded, waved good night to the receptionists, and walked out the door. There was something so beautiful and affirming about how this Black cemetery was also a bustling office. This place that, at times, held so much pain, this place where—nearly twenty-five years earlier—I had collapsed in tears, was also just a workplace. And not just any workplace, a workplace where people were happy, or so it seemed. This container built for pain also holds joy.

And why not? The lives of the people interred there had— one hoped—a mix of both. Was it reverent to shrink your feelings in their presence? Or could you laugh?

I walked out onto the grass, holding the map in my hand. They'd told me to look for a tree to orient myself and then to turn. This area of the cemetery was flat, with metal grave markers laid in verdant green lawns. I walked beside the main road, looking for the tree. All around me, dragonflies coasted low to the ground. I found what I thought was the tree and turned, but none of the numbers on the graves matched the grave-marker number I was looking for. I doubled back and tried again. I couldn't find it. The numbers were in a completely different sequence. I got overwhelmed by the immensity of the place. I didn't understand the system of organization, and I could wander all afternoon without knowing if I was getting any closer. I was out in the middle of a huge plot of land, and I was starting to get hot, and my frustration was quickly growing. The ease of the office had been a balm, but now I was left to my own devices and that was getting me nowhere.

I stopped and turned in a circle. I couldn't find it. I was lost and I had failed.

A Cadillac came rolling down the main road and stopped, idling. The nattily dressed older man rolled down the window and called out to me, "Do you need help, sir?"

He turned off his car and got out, spry and relaxed; his starched shirtsleeves were rolled up now. I apologized for taking up his time, but he waved it away. He said he was happy to help. I told him the grave-marker number and he told me I'd been heading in the wrong direction. I was heading away from the site the whole time.

He walked with me toward a tree line and pointed me toward the graves. He bent down and scraped dried mud off one of the corners. I noticed that there was a crack in my grandfather's grave marker, and I pointed it out. The older man apologized, looking perturbed.

"Please, if you have time, go into the office and tell them. They'll take care of it, sir. Thank you for noticing."

He wished me a good day, walked back to his car, and drove away.

I crouched down and let my fingers rest on the cracked marker.

My favorite of the photos my grandmother wrapped in Saran Wrap and thumbtacked to her wall finds her standing in front of a bus on a trip with friends from church. Her hand is on her hip, just below the cinched waist of her trench coat, her head thrown back—glamorous and cheeky. She looks confident and jubilant, unself-conscious and fully present. The destination displayed on the bus reads "Atlantic City." All my life I've thought about that trip to Atlantic City and what delights she must have found there and the memories she bound up in that photograph. I hope it was a wonderful day.

Alone outside, the smell of coconut and lime from the office was still in my nose, bright and rich. I considered the graves, their names—Adelita and Columbus—the dates, and the way that figures can never convey the fullness of the lives. The dragonflies coasted by, over the bright-green grass and beneath the electric-blue sky and all around me.

I wanted to call after the man's car as it drove away, my voice carrying on the wind: "Thank you. Thank you, sir, for seeing me. Thank you for caring for this site and for caring for these graves and for caring for me. I've been trying to dig myself out of this hole and I'm not there yet, but I know there is a light. Thank you for providing me a Black space to come to and for making it feel like home."

But he was gone now; the workday was over.

Clap Until You Feel It

Unfortunately, my life will always be a little bit incomplete because I will never be in the audience at an "Oprah's Favorite Things" show. For a brief, brilliant, beautiful period, it was one of the most deranged harbingers of the holiday season and a true source of joy. In the cupcake days in my twenties, while the annual televised holiday giveaways were still happening, I decided that once I got my life together, I would commit to the strategy required to figure out when the top-secret date of the taping would be and how to procure tickets. My life had gotten a little more together in the time since, but the "Favorite Things" shows had gotten away. Is it even Christmas if you're not looking under your seat and finding a new car?

As we neared our second Christmas in Baltimore, I set my sights on the holidays as an opportunity for a reset. I was trying to push back emotional darkness that was resistant to every attempted remedy. I kept thinking, *This, too, shall pass*. But, uh, shall it? I wanted a true source of joy; I wanted to be my own "Favorite Things" show. David and I decided that our apartment was a little too isolated and went in search of a new place to live, in a more active neighborhood. We wanted to see what else was possible for us in Baltimore. I was hopeful. The thing that I love about the Oprah Winfrey media empire and the "Favorite Things" show specifically is that it's all about possibility.

Even the act of trying to get to the "Favorite Things" show, not knowing which audience was going to receive the explosion of gifts, is freighted with possibility. All I want is possibility. I could feel it in the air as we moved into our new place. I could feel it like an audience member in the *Oprah* studio who notices an errant fake snowflake descending from the lighting grid a couple of seconds before the reveal.

One day I told David, "I think it'll be nice to get our first Christmas tree in the new apartment." He looked at me strangely.

"We got a Christmas tree last year," he said. "We went out to Valley View Farms, and they cut it down and we put it on top of your car." I had no memory of it at all. I searched my phone for pictures. I hadn't taken any. The whole first Christmas had disappeared into the darkness I'd been living in. I feared I was worse off than I thought. It wasn't just that sometimes I felt like I was pushing through a fog, but days of my life were fading into nothing.

David was concerned, but he didn't press it. Everything was going to change. Everything was possible. Our new apartment, in a neighborhood called Remington, was near to a bustling food hall; a theater company I was interested in working with; one of my favorite independent bookstores, Greedy Reads; and the Baltimore Museum of Art. It had big windows that faced an enclosed courtyard, and soon after we moved in, one of our neighbors stopped me in the hall and said that she read my column on *ELLE.com*. I was like, "Finally, a building with taste!"

I threw myself into work, taking on more responsibility at the website even as the political environment made it sometimes harder to find lightness for my column. I branched out to writing profiles and features on a regular basis. I tried to lean into curiosity as a way to keep the darkness at bay. My biggest opportunity came when my editor secured an interview with Wendy Williams and asked me to write a profile. Wendy is not Oprah, nor was she trying to be, but I was curious about her because she'd also built a powerful place in daytime television on the strength of her personality. Wendy's audience went wild in a way that was almost as vociferous as the "Oprah's Favorite Things" audience that I remembered so well and envied so deeply. I was curious about why that was. I wondered why the people who loved her loved her so intensely. I wanted to know how she really felt. The way I understand the world is through the lens of pop culture most of the time. These questions were about me as much as they were about her and the show. And so I went to New York to get answers.

I arrived at the studio at 9 A.M., wearing a sports coat and a button-down, with a pair of slacks; I brought a notebook and two mini-tape recorders just in case. If you've ever seen *The Wendy Williams Show,* you know that people came dressed like they were hitting the club right after; I looked like I was about to break Watergate. I was trying to convey professionalism and maybe a touch of style, but I realized, as the empty studio began to fill up with women in tiaras and four-inch heels, mom-and-daughter duos from the Midwest, gay men in muscle shirts, that I'd forgotten that this was supposed to be fun.

We were all quickly reminded of that fact by the show's hype man, Marco G, who came bounding out from backstage as a DJ spun hip-hop at top volume from huge speakers. Marco G raced up to a woman in the front row and bellowed, "ARE YOU READY?" She said yes. I was not.

Marco G demanded we all get up on our feet and start clapping to the beat. I put my little notebook under my chair. I was not aware there would be a participation segment. He ran us through a series of increasingly grueling warm-up exercises. We had to shout out our best "How you doin'?", Wendy's catchphrase; we had to put our arm around the person next to us, high-five the person in front of us, turn around and scream in the face of the person behind us. He wanted us to sit down. He wanted us to stand back up! He wanted us to clap! Harder! He needed us to clap harder! And he couldn't hear us scream! He needed to hear us scream! I had sweat pouring down my face; next to me was a white-haired woman in her sixties with her arm in a sling, who was outpacing me by every measure. "WHO NEEDS A DRINK?!" Marco G yelled at 9:45 A.M. Eastern Standard Time.

This is how you make daytime television, I realized. It isn't that the big emotional responses you sometimes see aren't real, but you have to get them to come out. I wondered what kind of hype person drove the frenzy train at *Oprah*. What kind of pre-show Barry's Bootcamp primes an audience for total and complete meltdown when presented with the enormity of possibility?

A few years back, I'd landed an audition for a game show. This was when I was still living in Philly and working at a university. The audition was over Zoom, and I called in from my office at work at the end of the day because it was the only slot the producer had available. The producer was a twenty-something guy, sitting in his apartment. That was surprising to me in the pre-COVID times. I guess I expected he'd be phoning in from the set or something. Spinning a big wheel and holding a skinny microphone. He looked like he'd just come from the gym and talked like he couldn't have cared less about me or my desire for cash and prizes. We played through a couple practice rounds of the game. He told me to act as excited or as bummed as I would on TV. I did my best to pretend to be a version of me who had solved a puzzle. Sitting in my office chair, trying not to be so loud as to alert the other people in the department that I was trying to win a fake ten thousand dollars instead of sending a spreadsheet to the registrar, I performed utter despondence over missing a clue. The twenty-something producer seemed ambivalent about my emotional whiplash.

"Okay," he sighed after a few rounds. "Now we're going to play the final clue. If you get it, I want you to go completely crazy, like you've won all the money."

I backed my office chair up to give room to the depths of emotion. I solved the clue correctly.

"Go nuts," he said.

I pumped my arms in the air. "Woo-hoo!" I cried, at a normal office volume.

I did not get on the show.

At *Wendy*, Marco was followed by Suzanne, a producer who was equally interested in hearing us scream. My voice was hoarse, but after watching Marco race up and down the stairs, bound down aisles, and run twerk contests for half an hour, I was fully committed to giving them whatever they needed. Suzanne was there to teach us how to respond. She was going to be standing right next to the camera and we were to look at her, not the camera, and do what she did. When she laughed, we were supposed to laugh. When she was shocked, we should also clutch our pearls. She told us she needed to make sure we could do it. She gave us a "Ha-ha-HA!" We went, "Ha-ha-HA!" She looked at Marco G; Marco G approved of our joy. Thank God—I would have been crushed if what we'd submitted was rejected! Suzanne screwed her face up in a scowl and made a demonstrative disapproving noise; we went, "Harrumph harrumph!" Marco G nodded again, another satisfactory emotional offering. This went on for ten minutes, and then it was time for the show to start. *Now* a show? I was *spent*. I was soaked through to the bone with sweat. I needed to sit down. I needed a therapist. I needed an exorcist. I hadn't stopped clapping for sixty minutes. My palms burned like I'd exfoliated with sandpaper.

Onstage, the *Wendy Williams Show* logo parted in the middle, and Wendy Williams, at last, walked out. She asked us, "How you doin'?"

We responded, "WE DON'T KNOW! WE'VE BEEN THROUGH A LOT!"

I have always thought of the "Favorite Things" audience as a group of people experiencing something almost traumatically wonderful, and I wanted that in the way that some people want the thrill of tornado chasing. It had been so long since I felt that. Think about the *joy*. That was the point of the whole thing, really, the joy of giving. Well, also, it's the joy that things can bring. But I do believe that, over the course of the fifteen years she was hosting "Favorite Things" shows, Oprah and her team did their best to make it a neutral good focused on altruism. One year the audience was all teachers; another year it was composed of people who had been affected by Hurricane Katrina. Once, during the recession, they highlighted free or inexpensive gifts, prioritizing human connection over stuff. I low-key would have been a little miffed about that, I gotta say. I read that folks left with one gratitude journal, end of list. Can you imagine? Honestly, what a serve. Oprah's like, "IT'S MY

'FAVORITE THINGS' SHOW!" and everyone faints from joy and rolls in the aisles. And then she says, "And my favorite thing is . . . the goodness in your own life! Everyone, I want to give you PERSPECTIVE!" I would have cackled. I would have gotten up off the floor, dusted off my T-shirt that read, "ALL I WANT FOR CHRISTMAS IS EVERYTHING," and I would have applauded her. What a fabulous episode of MTV's *Punk'd*. Now, where's all the stuff?

Yes, I do regret that I'll never get the things—the Allspice Cinnamon Powder Sugar Soak and the Sony VAIO S260 notebook computer and the panini press and the *Greatest Showman* original motion-picture soundtrack CD—but mostly what I was after in the early cupcake days and in these confounding new Baltimore days was the joy. But "joy" is too small a word. I reached for something bigger, seismic. The unbridled, deranged ecstasy of the experience. A feeling akin to sitting in that studio and discovering, along with three hundred other people in the same instant, that you were not only in the presence of Oprah but in the presence of her things, her favorite things. That you, by chance and luck and the intricacies of a production meeting held six to nine months ago, have been chosen. That, yes, you may need to pay the taxes on the loot you tote home and, yes, you may not even want some of these things, but for this one moment everything aligned for you. *For you!* That you are, perhaps, one of those favorite things by extension. That's good. That's chaotic good.

Look under your seat: Your best life is emerging.

I love to watch "Favorite Things" videos on YouTube, but most of the clips aren't even about the stuff, which is fine with me. I don't watch for the stuff. I watch for the chaos. I watch them because they're like Beyoncé concerts or like tent revivals or like that moment when Tom Hanks made fire in *Cast Away*. It's a spectacle. It's wild to watch; like, "Wow, these people are really going through it." But it wakes something up in me, too.

I have a whole playlist of videos that make me feel something incredible and extreme. Fantasia Barrino singing "I'm Here" from *The Color Purple,* also on *Oprah,* or the video from post-show karaoke at the Broadway show *Waitress* when a kid shocked everyone with a heart-wrenching rendition of "She Used to Be Mine," or a clip of Debra Winger saying goodbye to her kids in *Terms of Endearment.* Some of these videos— I'll admit—I watch because I feel like being sad. Even in okay times, there is a subterranean river of melancholy in me, and sometimes a productive afternoon is comprised of using You-Tube videos of varying qualities like divining rods. I watch these videos, some of which I could recite by heart, and I find the mouth of the river and I stoop down and place my hands in the sadness and it feels like, God, it feels like the truth. It feels like *finally.* It feels like for a moment I don't have to walk around this world all neutral. Because as much as I was struggling, I didn't look any different to the world. And sometimes when you don't look different, you start to think maybe it's not real. Maybe you're faking it or deceiving yourself. Maybe this is just what neutral feels like.

But this world is not neutral, and I am not neutral, and as many times as I send my little emails using an appropriate number of exclamation points—but not! Too! Many.—and have small talk with Uber drivers and try to remember if I've watered the plants or taken my pills or eaten, I still always have the thought, *Can anybody see what's really happening here?* Which is to say, aren't we all human people walking around with all of our experiences, all of our sadness and joy and grief and hope and fear, barely contained by our skin and our adherence to decorum? I'm not saying I want to walk around all the time *feeling* publicly, but it seems a waste of life to never go to the depths and see what's there. And what's there is the truth, and sometimes the truth is sad. Other times, the truth is the deranged joy of the 2012 video where Ton Do-Nguyen made a shot-for-shot recreation of Beyoncé's "Countdown" video while wearing a Snuggie. And still other times the truth is the mad exuberance of the reveal moment on an old episode of "Oprah's Favorite Things." That's what the poet means when he says we contain multitudes. In these *Oprah* videos, you see the recognition wash over the faces of the audience members when she tells them what the show's theme is, and you know that they are experiencing something so extreme and good that they will probably remember the shock of it for the rest of their lives. And don't we all want the shock of the extremely good?

There's one video I love from 2010, the year that she did two full shows of "Favorite Things." There was so much bounty in the world then, it overflowed to the next day. At the start of the episode, she really hoodwinks the audience. You can tell that they are hoping against hope that they've lucked into the show. They already know they've been given tickets because they've all done kind things for others, and sometimes a ticket to *Oprah* is enough of a reward for altruism. But they're hoping for more. You can see it on their faces, the raised eyebrows of anticipation, the slightly agape mouths, the way that they're listening so hard but they're not hearing a thing. They're in the presence of Oprah—so close; it's a smaller audience that year—and yet their minds are on another planet.

Oprah, in a black dress with a wide swatch of yellow across the middle, stands on a darkened stage in front of two black leather chairs. She starts talking about how important giving is, and you can feel the blood pressure of every audience member spike, even through the screen, even all these years later. But Oprah glides right past it, reminding them that they've all given of themselves and they've been brought here to talk about it. She gestures to a chair. They all remember some conversation they've had with a producer at some point. They all think that they're going to be sitting across from Oprah, talking, and, yes, that, too, is its own reward. But they're still hoping for more.

Then Oprah starts talking about meditation, and everyone in the audience just slightly deflates. This is the subject of the show, they think. And, frankly, it seems like a really overstuffed program. All these people are going to tell their stories and then Dr. Phil or someone is going to talk about breathing in through your nose and out through your mouth? It's going to be a long afternoon.

Oprah says, "The truth is that when you meditate, it allows you to . . . clear a channel for giving, giving to others. So how about we meditate on this?" Suddenly bells start jingling, and *then* Oprah Winfrey, Queen of Television, reaches behind her back and *rips off the black dress*, exposing a festive red dress with a bedazzled neckline. *Oprah does a reveal like she's on RuPaul's Drag Race!* TENS ACROSS THE BOARD. And the people in the audience *lose their minds*. One woman holds up both hands and rocks back and forth with her eyes closed like she is in full praise mode; another bends over and starts wailing while gripping both of her hands together so tight that they must have ached for days; a man in a black suit hops up, screams like he's in a horror movie, and then topples over. When have you ever in your life?!

Fake snow starts falling and people are still screaming, jumping up and down, crying. Their mouths are pulled out at odd angles because the sounds they're making are too big for the body to handle. A blond man collapses onto a chair, one hand gripping the railing in front of him while the other covers his red, tear-soaked face. He cannot control himself. That's how happy. That's how much joy. They are embracing each other and sobbing like they all just survived a plane crash. This goes on for a full minute. Screaming! Pulling their hair out at the roots on television! One woman has somehow procured a tissue box and is dabbing her eyes. Where did the tissues come from?! We love a prepared queen! We love prop comedy! These people are dressed in their heterosexual best, and yet they are giving full drag-show antics. Why *wouldn't* I watch this every day?

If you've seen the *Saturday Night Live* sketch gently mocking the "Favorite Things" show, you probably remember that during the audience's excitement, a woman goes into labor, Tina Fey goes feral and starts eating a gift turkey, and Amy Poehler's head explodes. I'd bet that that sketch is more clearly remembered than any one "Favorite Things" response from real life. But what's apparent every time I watch the real thing is that the sketch was not exaggerating in the least.

At the minute mark, Oprah is clapping gamely as she watches a room full of people have nervous breakdowns. Somehow, I think that this is part of just being Oprah. And I wonder what it's like to live the kind of life where your presence sometimes inspires people to burst into tears, shout, and collapse in front of you, while you wait patiently.

Oprah starts talking, trying to move the show along. But the revival isn't over yet. A woman with fake snow in her hair says to her friend, "I'm going to drop dead"; you can read it clearly on her lips. And you sort of believe her. The man in the black suit who fell over is on the ground on his knees, clapping and rocking. This is church. This is a concert. This is one of those videos of a soldier coming home from war and greeting his dog. This is Tandi Iman Dupree dressed like Wonder Woman, dropping from the ceiling of an event hall onto the stage in a full split. This is the finale of *Lost,* because, spoiler alert, they've all passed on and gone to glory.

It is the most unhinged thing I have ever seen. I watched it all the time in that second Baltimore apartment. And I felt, for a moment, alive.

"Oprah's Favorite Things" is theater. And I love theater. It's the doo-wop girls swelling to a gospel-tinged crescendo as Audrey and Seymour belt "Suddenly Seymour." It's the sound engineer on the *Ragtime* original Broadway cast recording punching Audra McDonald's mic up to eleven for the high note at the end of the opening number. It's Nettie and Celie reuniting after all those long years apart in *The Color Purple.* It's what I buy my ticket for—that intensity, that magic. Theater is the palace of Big Feelings. There, in the dark, all that swirls within us is set loose in the air using monologues and music. Why would you ever want to be anywhere else? I think that's what life is really about—the moments where the mics get turned up to eleven. Everything else is just stuff.

I'm sure there was a hype person for the audience at *Oprah* like there was at *The Wendy Williams Show.* Maybe their tactics were different—switch out the hip-hop for Tina Turner, maybe; no twerk contest—but the end goal is the same: an audience full of people who are a hair's breadth away from frenzy. It's like anti-yoga. Do not center yourself; do not listen to your breathing; do not let the soft animal of your body love what it loves. Not right now. Now is the time to love everything around you all at once. I think that's beautiful. I like going to yoga, but

I think I'd enjoy a session in an anti-yoga studio. I'm picturing something like that orb that Jodie Foster gets tossed around in at the end of *Contact*. Truly, that's what these audiences have just endured minutes before the cameras roll on a talk-show episode. They're shaking, they're crying, they're shouting to the control room: "I'm okay to go! I'm okay to go!" And, as in *Contact,* on the other side of it: heaven.

I kept looking for my version of the talk-show pre-show or the *Contact* orb in Baltimore. Something to shake me out of the gray version of myself. The new apartment was better, but—this will shock you—things will not solve your problems. Even if those things are real estate! I tried yoga, I tried the gym, I tried social mixers. Nothing came of it. The malaise had grown into a big feeling, a dark feeling, an aggressively nothing feeling. I'd expected, upon moving back, to be in a fight with Baltimore and the vestiges of my past there. I did not expect what actually happened: Baltimore presented itself to me as a vibrant, interesting city that I couldn't figure out how to access. I wanted something more than this. I wanted a psychological hype person.

I decided that maybe I should get some more help. In addition to seeing my therapist, I started going to a psychiatrist whom I'd heard about from a friend. I called her at 7 P.M. on a weeknight, expecting to get an office voicemail, but instead she picked up right away and gave me an address in Mount Vernon. She told me to come the following Friday. On Friday, I reported not to an office but to an old townhouse in Baltimore City that was, by all appearances, someone's home. I rang the doorbell. A harried white man opened a huge wooden door with wrought-iron bars on the window.

"I'm here to see the psychiatrist," I said tentatively.

"Do you have an appointment?" he asked. I told him I did. He disappeared for a moment, leaving me on the stoop, then he came back to the door. "Sorry, she's double-booked. Just wait a minute."

Finally, the door opened, another patient walked out, and I was led through a dark vestibule, past a grand staircase, and into a parlor full of file cabinets and one small desk. The man from the door sat on the edge of the desk, next to a jar full of loose change. He asked me for my visit fee (as you may already be surmising, she did not take insurance); I paid it. I kept thinking, *Is this legal?* But then I would think, *Well, even if it's not, I haven't done anything wrong. I'm just sad. And if it's illegal to be sad in America, everybody is going to jail.*

I was ushered into a smaller room behind the parlor, where every surface was covered in paper. I sat at a desk in front of a small, bespectacled woman who looked a bit like a *Cathy* cartoon. This was the psychiatrist. And she was—I checked—licensed and accredited and in good standing, even though her whole operation felt a little bit like a Gilded Age drug deal. One opium, please, madam. She asked me what I was there for. I talked to her about how I was feeling hopeless. She asked me how I wanted to feel. I looked for a camera and a producer off to the side to tell me what I should be emoting. No dice.

When you show up to *Oprah*, even if you're not expecting the "Favorite Things," there's a part of you that's been primed by everything about Oprah to believe that you're going to come away from this experience better, fuller, more in touch with your best life. That's the whole ethos. You tell yourself even being in her presence will make you a more self-actualized person. You hype yourself up just by requesting the ticket or flying to Chicago. And there's a way of thinking that says that this works, too. If you believe you are going to be better, you will in some way get better. The psychiatrist asked me how I wanted to feel, and I said, "Better?" but what was true was that I wanted to feel like I believed better was possible.

Two opiums, please.

She rustled through some papers, some of which definitely had other people's personal information on them, and found a scrap. She drew me a chemical compound. I stared at it. She wrote down some side effects. I nodded. She wrote me a prescription for an antidepressant and sent me on my way. The whole thing took ten minutes.

I started taking the antidepressant, having talked about the visit and the medical interactions with my primary-care physician and my therapist. Everyone agreed that the process was shady as hell but the pills were fine, which is about the best you can expect from drugs. After about a month, I realized that I struggled to care about anything. I was still doing my job writing comedy, I was working on my book, I was existing in the world, but nothing mattered. Nothing made a blip on my radar. Everything was a basic flatness—nothing great, nothing bad. This was a change from before, as I'd felt depression weighing everything down like a blanket, so even the happy things were sepia-toned. Now I just hung out in the middle. None of my feelings were big. I didn't know if that was better.

I went back to the psychiatrist. The man at the door was once again surprised to see me.

"Do you have an appointment?" he asked.

"Sir," I said, "can you all switch to Outlook or something? I'm really struggling here."

Inside, the psychiatrist looked at me, puzzled, as I relayed my new symptoms—the malaise, the apathy. She rustled some papers. She definitely had mad-genius vibes, which was comforting, I guess. When you're trying to fix your brain, you don't want to work with a mad idiot. She drew another chemical compound. She asked me if I wanted to try a different medication or a different dose to get me out of my medically induced ambivalence. I said, "You'll be shocked to hear this, but I don't give a shit."

She changed the prescription. I went away for a few weeks and tested it out. I didn't really feel much different, which is to say I still didn't really feel. It came time for me to go back. I called to schedule an appointment, and she confirmed me for the next week. I showed up on the date and time of the appointment and found that nobody was home. I thought, *Well, what now?*

My pills ran out eventually and, after talking with my doctor and my therapist, I decided to try something different and went off antidepressants. The feelings got bigger, and for a while they got dark again, which worried me. Was this who I would be forever? I didn't know, and so I just kept doing what I knew how to do. I went to work, I wrote my column, I went to therapy, I watched TV with David, I tried to reach out. I waited. I kept looking up for the errant snowflake. The sign of possibility. The harbinger of joy.

I thought of Oprah at the "Favorite Things" show in 2010, in that split second where she's clapping and watching, a smile frozen on her face as everyone around her goes mad with joy. I wondered if she ever felt the disconnect between *being* her show and being *at* her show. I'll bet her mind wandered in those moments, back to her own life, away from the theater of it all. Maybe in her mind she's in her garden, or mentally composing an email, or remembering something that happened forty years ago when she'd first started her career anchoring the six o'clock news in Baltimore. I wondered what it was like to be at work while everyone else was having the biggest feelings of their lives.

I'm not depressed, I would think while typing up jokes for my audience of internet people. *I'm just like Oprah*.

Early in the fall, I went to the opening night of a musical at Baltimore Center Stage called *Miss You Like Hell* by Quiara Alegría Hudes and Erin McKeown. It follows a mother and daughter, one a U.S. citizen and the other an undocumented immigrant from Mexico, on a circuitous cross-country journey to reunite and stay reunited, despite the threat of the United States immigration system. It was phenomenal—beautiful and funny and heart-wrenching. During the last song, the immensity of what was happening hit me so hard that I felt a wail rising up in me, and I put my head down in my hands to squelch it. I was embarrassed by my response, even though it was a right one, so I tried to make myself small.

After the musical was over and the cast had taken their bows, I sat back down in the emptying theater, lowered my head into my lap, and I cried and I cried. This emotion had been working its way out for a long time, and it had a long way to travel. I couldn't outrun it anymore. I was grateful for it, grateful to the play, for giving me such big feelings in a way that made sense. I'd spent so long feeling bottled up and weighed down, afraid of the feelings that were clouding my life. Finally, something connected.

In the lobby, I met up with friends at the opening-night reception. "I cried so hard!" I told them, pointing at my still-wet eyes. "I cried!" I said, wanting to express how deeply the musical had affected me and desperate to have a moment where I wasn't walking around this world all neutral. I want to be unguarded and open because theater, like joy, like life, is ephemeral, and I won't pass this way again.

I am not made smaller by the big feelings. They are the things that remind me that I am alive. They are the things that, when I'm in darkness, remind me that I'm searching for the light. They aren't always the things that I need, but I think that inside them—the happiness, the sadness, the joy, the grief—there is truth. I just want to get to the truth. I write to get to the truth. I watch to see the truth. I go to the theater to find the truth. I laugh and I cry and I gasp. And at the end, I clap and I clap and I clap until my hands hurt.

Break Room Cake Communion

"What if you joined a co-working space?" Brian asked. Our therapy sessions had pivoted, after a year or so, to figuring out ways for me to form new community connections. So I did it. I found a co-working space. I paid my membership fee. I put on a jaunty outfit that said, "I am cultured but also I will gossip with you." I brought my laptop to the sleekly redesigned space in downtown Baltimore and got ready to be inundated with friends, associates, work spouses, and, I suppose, co-workers, if absolutely necessary. And you know what I found, at this co-working space? A bunch of people sitting around all day in silence, doing their jobs.

I'd been bamboozled.

This is not a problem with the co-working space or the advice, per se. It's not like they advertised themselves as the adult Chuck E. Cheese I'd hoped for. I don't fault these people for just wanting a place to connect to Wi-Fi and prepare spreadsheets or whatever it is people do at their jobs. And, to be fair, they did have "beer and movie" nights at the co-working space. And sometimes a few people would make slightly burnt popcorn in the afternoon and talk very quietly in the kitchen area. I think there was some kind of "run club" (unclear from what). But after a couple of days sitting alone at a long white table smiling benignly into the middle distance like I was manning a booth at a job fair, I had to admit that perhaps I'd entered into this working relationship with the wrong intentions. Like a contestant on a dating show already planning their post-show pivot to Instagram influencer, I was not here for the right reasons. I didn't want to work at the co-working space; I don't even want to work at the working space. I wanted to hang out.

When I would visit the *ELLE* office in New York, I'd spend an entire day talking with my co-workers, planning with my editor, making cappuccino in the sun-drenched break room with the Smeg fridge full of gifted wine, shopping for promotional swag on the free table, and going to pitch meetings, which are hangouts with agendas. I was so delighted to have the opportunity for social interaction, to talk about ideas, to be in the thrall of my witty, brilliant co-workers, that I rarely got any of the actual writing part of my job done. Who wants to type on a laptop when you can talk to the arbiters of taste and culture? After I left the office on my intermittent visits, I'd find a seat in the café car of an evening train back to Baltimore and set up a little productivity station. Speeding back southward, I'd rush to catch up on my writing, never more inspired and excited to work.

I wrote some of my best stuff in moving vehicles. On a train, I wrote a popular column about Leslie Jones turning a Christian Siriano fashion show into a tent revival; I wrote about Beyoncé's stunningly rococo second pregnancy photo shoot from a bus; and when Congresswoman Maxine Waters faced down former Treasury secretary Steve Mnuchin, instantly popularizing the procedural phrase "reclaiming my time," I got so hype that I pulled my car over, parked in the lot of an Arby's, and climbed into the back seat to write. Maybe I didn't need an office, I needed a fleet.

At the co-working space, I'd spend my days ping-ponging through the open floor plan, always moving—a shark, hunting for camaraderie. I'd approach serious-looking nonprofit administration types and ask, "Do you want to be friends?!"

And they'd reply, "Not now, babe, I'm participating in the economy."

I mean, me, too. But that doesn't mean we can't spend an hour and a half exchanging personal anecdotes that slowly but surely hint at the vastness of our inner lives. Why else have a job? I want to work. I just don't want to work at work.

I started dreading going to the co-working space. And I'd feel bad about dreading it. The co-working space was very nice! But in the mornings, I'd still struggle to tumble out of bed and stumble to the kitchen, pouring myself a cup of ambition even though I knew I'd buy another cup at the co-working space in exchange for a few precious minutes of light banter with the barista. I'd sit in my car after my five-minute commute, psyching myself up to go in. I had taken all the worst parts about having a job and decided I should also pay for them. So I canceled my membership.

"Don't worry about throwing me a going-away party," I'd say to the stressed nonprofit administrator types as we were waiting in line for the coffee counter.

"I don't know who you are," they'd reply.

"Okay, but you *could*."

You know what I'd like? I'd like to work in a fake office. More *Truman Show* than the TV show *Severance*, I think. Everyone else could be doing a job, like a functional office. I guess. I mean, I don't care. I don't want any responsibilities for that mess. The work-product stuff. I'm just here for perks. All I want are the ancillary benefits of being in an office. Things like going-away parties and low-stakes gossip and chatting about what TV you watched and—the golden goose of office work— free cake in the break room. In every office I've worked, word of complimentary cake races through the ranks of the cubicle class like it's a rumor about the Wells Fargo wagon showing up in River City, Iowa. Free break room cake is a blessing, a gift from some benevolent force that asks nothing of you in return. Free break room cake offers you an opportunity to share a portion of some other person's joy, both literally and figuratively. In a space built on capitalist power structures, free break room cake reminds you that you don't need to produce anything to be deserving of a little sweetness.

I've worked my fair share of pure-drudgery office jobs—low pay, abusive managers, atrocious interior design. I did not love them. But I was always fascinated by them. Sometimes it was the aghast fascination one has with utter tackiness. Other times, it was the fascination that comes from being plunged into another world that runs on its own rules and traditions, almost disconnected from reality. At one office, a law firm in Philadelphia where I worked as a legal assistant for a year, we weren't allowed to speak. Our jobs—processing the various components of mortgage foreclosures, bleak work—were considered so rote that there was little reason to converse. Our verbalized thoughts got in the way of productivity. If we did need to get feedback from a manager, we could go to their office and break the vow of silence. But the little clusters of assistants plugging away at never-ending spreadsheets of dreams deferred had no need for voice or interiority; we were just the work. I found that fascinating. I also found it fascinating that we could listen to music or podcasts using headphones, perhaps to further encourage us not to speak.

This was a place where the powers that be had spent an inordinate amount of time designing methods of control, order, and obedience. I have never worked in a space with a darker energy. I found that fascinating! Although I hated it and their hair-trigger sensitive late policy and the casual racism of two of the partners, I loved how the specific, desperate, delightful weirdness of humans in an office broke through.

And *of course* the people in my cluster—eight college-educated twenty-somethings shoved into an office designed for four people—became friends. We'd slip off our headphones and whisper anecdotes to each other, as if our weekend plans and our opinions on *Grey's Anatomy* were wartime spy codes. We'd send a lookout to the doorway and then swivel our chairs around and crane our necks beyond our monitors and hang out. We'd get into petty arguments and share gossip from other clusters, and two of us started dating and then quickly stopped dating, which was a mess. A wonderful mess. A blessed mess. And occasionally one of us would slip to the break room long enough to feel human again but not so long that human resources would send a warning email about violating the amount of time allowed for being away from one's desk without clocking out. At just under seven minutes, the emissary would slip back into the cluster, type a few strokes on their keyboard so the inactivity sensor wouldn't go off, and then whisper to the rest of us, "There's cake!"

I had ended up in this soul-sucking silent situation the way everyone ends up here: chasing a dollar. Two years earlier, I'd found the move from waiting tables to restaurant management to be a bad fit. I loved waiting tables. I loved the aggressive, angry, delightful hanging out of being on a service staff at a busy restaurant. I loved having small interactions with people I would never see again. I loved talking about food. And I usually loved the money. But it wasn't consistent, of course. And while struggling to make ends meet at a Rittenhouse Square restaurant that was undergoing a midlife crisis, I began exploring the possibility of something more stable. Management work was objectively more hours, and every moment of hanging out was infused with a responsibility to, like, manage. But the paycheck was the same every week, there was health insurance, and I decided those were things that would improve my life.

I wasn't wrong, per se. Health insurance and a steady paycheck are, shockingly, great for one's quality of life. It's just everything else about the job that was a bad fit. So I left the restaurant industry and, through a friend, found a job working as a legal assistant at a firm in New Jersey. I liked the Jersey firm a lot, but then I got greedy. I was making $12.75 an hour, and there was a notoriously draconian Philadelphia firm that was offering $13.75 an hour. One dollar more. It was, to me, a fortune.

I thought about that New Jersey office all the time, though. I mean, what else did I have to do? Sitting at my desk in my quiet cluster, sous-vide-ing in silence. The New Jersey law firm couldn't have been more different from the Philly one. The Jersey office was an extremely social space, a vibe that started with the management team, all of whom were related and saw no reason to leave family business at the door. The workload was the same, but talking was almost required. The year leading up to my boss's wedding to her boss was absolutely thrilling, as it featured near-daily updates about the guest list and menu and conflicts and fears. At one point, my boss's mom, her aunt, her sister, and her grandmother (all employees) brought in the dresses they were wearing to the wedding and walked through the aisles between cubicles, showing them off for those of us who weren't invited. It was incredible.

This was still an office, but it was also, crucially, a hangout. I was delighted. The New Jersey firm had an office culture like the one in *9 to 5* after Franklin Hart gets kidnapped. It was just so full of life, much of which was absolutely nonsense. People's desks were covered with photos and magazine cutouts and random toys and inside jokes. One co-worker and I got into a prank war, where the only weapon was mailing each other photos of the Jonas Brothers, using the firm's office supplies and postage from the mailroom. Everyone was always selling popcorn or pizza or cookies to support their kids' social lives. We dressed up for Halloween and for the office Olympics and for Christmas.

Unsurprisingly, this was also an office that had a huge capacity for the kind of distracting nonsense that makes a workday bearable—there was cake *constantly*. I presume they made money somehow. Although a google search indicates that the firm abruptly went out of business in 2018. But surely it wasn't due to office shenanigans. The shenanigans were the whole point. Capitalism is built on shenanigans!

The Baltimore County office where Brian did therapy was restructuring. This meant new job responsibilities for him and a move to a different building. The new location was a longer drive for me, but, like, what else was I doing? We'd been working together for nearly two years, and I'd experienced a profound change in my emotional state during that time. It occurred so slowly I didn't notice it for a while. Which is, I guess, how therapy works, but I'm a real abracadabra queen, so this shocked me. I came in lamenting my old life, and then I spent a long period miserably trying to reckon with my new life, but lately I was asking the question, "What am I trying to make of myself, my time, and my work going forward?" I'd started to believe in possibility, and belief led to action, and action led to movement. It helped, of course, that I was working with someone who was kind and patient, who was well trained, and who was fascinated enough by my job to let me start sessions saying things like "Okay, so I wrote this humor column about Anthony Scaramucci but an actual congressperson slid into my DMs to ask me a serious question about it and I was like, 'I'm a clown, babe, I don't have the answers you seek. Also, shouldn't you be running the government right now? Who is minding the Liberty Bell or whatever?' So, was that the right response?"

Brian still maintained that he didn't google me or read my work, so as to free me to be my whole self in our sessions. Outrageous! But through our conversations I was able to mentally unite two things that had once seemed at odds: my desire for community and my love for the solitary profession I had. I felt seen and heard, and that allowed me the room to generate new ideas and approaches in a space that had felt so empty. It's remarkable what can come of a professional conversation.

Brian's new office had a computer because he had taken on more day-to-day managerial duties, which I intuited were stressful. He didn't overshare or make the time about him, but every once in a while I'd catch a stray detail in our conversations, and I'd snatch it out of the air and lock it away in my mind palace, because I am very nosy and I was desperate for office gossip.

Sometimes I would try to use the opening banter as a way of finding out what was going on. You know that thing where you start therapy with five minutes of light comedy to put everyone at ease before saying something like, "Well, anyway. I'm devastated"? I love that part. I call it the top-of-the-show monologue.

I don't really think therapy is a show, but I try to say deranged things at regular intervals so that my insurance will see fit to keep paying for it. And, even if you take therapy very seriously, which I do, the fact remains that there is nothing better than making your therapist laugh. That is not a pity laugh, and you know it because they are trained not to laugh. So anything that escapes is real, 100 percent pure mirth. Gold standard. A therapy laugh will gas me up for a week. Untouchable. Not a problem in sight.

One day, when I came in for a session, I noticed that Brian had changed the background on his office computer to a meme from *The Office*. I incorporated some of my thoughts on the sitcom into my top-of-the-show monologue and then seamlessly segued into a discussion about whether I should try to get my professional culture fix by hiring a virtual assistant. What would the assistant do? I wasn't sure. I moved on.

The next week, there was a different meme from *The Office* on his desktop. I didn't mention it, but I put it in the mind palace. The third week, there was yet another new meme. After a month of rotating office comedy content, I asked about it. I try not to ask questions in therapy other than "Can you please tell me exactly what to do?" And I never ask personal questions. But the memes were just looking right at me. And professionalism doesn't always have to leech selfhood, curiosity, or joy from us. Brian laughed and explained that when he got frustrated with some office drama, he would change his background to a meme that reflected the nature of his frustration. It was a small way of blowing off steam without bringing it into the workspace. I ate this information up like it was an entire sheet cake.

"But now that you've noticed it," he said, "I've got to keep changing them just to keep the pattern up." What a fun shenanigan we were sharing! I wanted office culture, but I would absolutely take *Office* culture instead.

A few more weeks passed, and each time I came in, there was a new *Office* meme. I'd chuckle about it and then we'd get down to business. Then one afternoon I came in and noticed that the meme hadn't changed. I pointed at the screen accusatorily before I even sat down.

"That's the same desktop from last week! What's wrong?"

Brian let out a pained sigh. "I forgot!" he cried, his Southern accent growing more intense. "It came to me as soon as they told me you were here, and I panicked. I thought about having them hold you in the waiting room, but that's just ridiculous." He put his head in his hand forlornly. He seemed deeply chagrined.

I looked at the screen: Steve Carell yelling, "Bankruptcy!" I looked at Brian: despondent. Now it was my turn to laugh, big and loud and genuine. I'd successfully managed to give my therapist anxiety. All in a day's work.

Another Person in the Room

One of the things they don't tell you is that making friends as an adult is so embarrassing. It doesn't seem like it's going to be such a big deal in the movies or on TV. The *Friends* were just sitting around and this deranged woman in a wedding dress comes in and starts ranting and they responded, "Would you like to hang out with us literally every moment for the next ten years and then marry one of us?" (And, yes, I know that Rachel knew Ross and Monica from before. I'm *aware*. Please don't email me about this. I'm just saying that when I put on the suit I bought for *my* wedding and started prognosticating at the coffee shop where everyone wore Carhartt jackets, they just turned the volume up on the record player and looked away. I went to the baristas and was like, "Do *you* want to be friends?" and they replied, "WE WERE ON A BREAK!")

I thought making adult friends was going to be all about running into some random acquaintance and going, "Hey there, Chuck, what say you and I hit the ole racquetball around at the club this weekend!" And instead it's me devoting a whole day to composing a text message that reads, "Dear neighbor, this is Eric! Please excuse the exclamation point. It works better in context. As you previously mentioned, you like events and occurrences, as do I. Would you like to co-attend this neutral event at a mutually agreeable time with me and perhaps have a conversation? Please let me know what your Outlook calendar tells you! Oh God! That exclamation point was a mistake! My shame! DELETE! DELETE!"

Even when you do manage to send the text about an adult-friends hang, the response is like, "Definitely! I'm free in six years. We should put it on the calendar now, because I'm going to lose that open slot quickly. Okay, amazing! See you then. I will definitely not be too tired when the time comes and politely ask to reschedule!"

I believe that some of the magic of friendship-building is proximity, which was one of the main impetuses behind the move to the second apartment. We were near a food hall and a CrossFit gym, both of which are like catnip to millennial adults. The building was in a more highly trafficked area; it wasn't a schlep for people to reach us, and it seemed likely that we'd be able to have the kind of casual run-ins that can, over time, accumulate into the holy grail of adult friendship: the "let's do something sometime!"

I love sometime! I am a big fan of doing something!

It's hard to figure out how much of adult friendship is about personality matches and how much is just logistics. When I learned how to make friends, in school and in college, everyone was just right there every day, and I had nothing else going on to preclude spending hundreds of hours together. The first time this didn't work was in sophomore year of college, when my freshman-year best friend told me he had to cut back on friendship to focus on his pre-med studies. Outwardly I was like, "I totally get it." Inwardly I cried, "AGH! I've been mortally wounded!" I had had friendships ebb and flow, of course, but I'd never encountered someone who expressed the need to prioritize another part of their lives so concretely. I was used to studying for the SATs until 2 A.M., talking on the phone the whole time. We could make this work! Anyway, he's a doctor now, so congratulations on that *choice,* I guess.

As you move into adulthood, so many more things take precedence, demand time and attention, and cloud your mental space. When I try to hang out with friends who have kids, for instance, I always say, "We can literally do this anytime, day or night. We can hang out at three-minute increments spread out over a week. We can wear pajamas; I will not have any opinions about the state of your house. Here is the number for my secret phone. When it feels like you might have time to do something together, just call once and hang up. I will be there in less than two minutes."

It can be done. But it takes effort. So much more effort than I'd ever had to put into it.

And I started to wonder if, after nearly two years in Baltimore, the effort was worth it. The paradox of making new friends as a married adult is that you have to lean into a space of incompleteness inside this life that is pretty complete, at least by the standards of rom-coms, fairy tales, and the timeless love story of Jim and Pam from *The Office.*

In the movie *Romy and Michele's High School Reunion,* the titular best friends memorably maintain a long-standing fight over which of them is the Mary, as in Mary Richards, the lead from *The Mary Tyler Moore Show.* Neither wants to be the Rhoda, her brash, unlucky-in-love neighbor. It's a shorthand for two people trying to claim agency after having been underdogs their whole lives. I get that. But I wondered if I was in a phase of life where I wanted to be the Rhoda. Sometimes you just want to show up, eat someone else's food, and bounce.

Mary could, as the theme song claimed, turn the world on with her smile, but Rhoda, infused with Valerie Harper's flinty energy, was the one who could give it to you straight. She was sometimes the confidante, sometimes the coach, and often the comparison—neurotically complaining about her weight or her love life to her seemingly more put-together friend. Rhoda is an anxious person who uses humor as a shield and a bridge at once. This, I understood deeply.

In the second episode of *The Mary Tyler Moore Show,* written by Treva Silverman, Rhoda gets herself into a typical pickle trying to set up a double date for herself and Mary. Mary's date is obsessed with Mary, as everyone seems to be. But when Rhoda calls to invite over a man she's met in passing, the man gladly accepts the invitation, then says he'll bring his wife. On the night of the get-together, feeling like a third wheel (or, really, fifth wheel), Rhoda buries herself in a bowl of chips. "Allow me to introduce myself," she declares to no response from Mary's besotted beau. "I'm another person in the room."

In therapy, Brian suggested I join an app to meet casual acquaintances. "Like Grindr?" I asked. He looked at me quizzically and clarified. It was called Bumble BFF; it was a section of a dating app specifically designed for people who wanted to make friends. I made a profile and did what I used to do on dating apps: shared way too much and injected so much personality into the "About Me" section that I seemed deranged. "Allow me to introduce myself," I wrote. "I'm another person in the room."

Shockingly, very few people responded. Didn't anybody watch Nick at Nite in the nineties? Most of what I found on the app were straight couples who lived outside DC, looking for hiking buddies. This was a bridge too far. I hadn't been willing to go on a hike to get dates, and I certainly wasn't willing to traverse nature in order to build a third-wheel friendship with a political analyst and a development director living in Silver Spring.

I'd wager that, as part of our effort to expand our friend group during those first couple of years in Baltimore, David and I were introduced to 60 percent of the interracial gay couples in the city and surrounding areas. The other 40 percent were actively avoiding us, I suppose. It wasn't that people were purposefully setting us up on friend dates with other interracial gay couples, although I do think that would be hilarious. "Here, you guys sit at this pizza restaurant and discuss how you had very different reactions to the film *BlacKkKlansman*!" Instead, I think the meetups were random and perhaps stick in my memory only because they were interracial gay relationships and not, like, boring-ass same-sames. By the by, it would be hilarious if we required people in non-interracial relationships to call themselves same-sames. Let's commit to this. For justice.

Like, you meet the white boyfriend of your white co-worker at the Christmas party and you exclaim, "Oh! I didn't know your boyfriend was white! What is it like being same-sames?"

And your co-worker replies, "We're just two people. We don't really think about what it's like to be . . . as you said, same-sames."

And you pour yourself another eggnog and grab a cookie that's supposedly shaped like a reindeer but actually looks like the state of Michigan. "Yeah, but in this climate? It's very brave. Do your parents all get along? What do you think your kids are going to look like?"

I really don't walk around this great big world actively pondering the interraciality of my relationship. I think that would stress me out. I think it would break our humanness down into pieces. I think it would frame who we are and are trying to be, as a unit, in the wrong way. Do I sometimes point out that my husband is white? Sure, but I mostly do that for comedy reasons. We're not together because of what our races are. Both of us have done plenty of same-same dating in the past. And I've found that when I meet other couples who are of different races, we hardly ever discover that we all share some deeper understanding of life or love or the Civil Rights Act of 1964 simply by virtue of who we're filing taxes with. This isn't to say it doesn't matter. It matters, it all matters. It shows up in every facet of our lives. But just as I'm unclear what people mean when they ask me about the Black Experience, I am not so sure that there is a singular or even collective Interracial Relationship Experience. I didn't get the minutes from the Swirl Agenda meeting. So we're just winging it.

There was one couple we met, however, that I thought might have a unique insight into the life that David and I were building. They were also gay, one Black man and one white, and the white member of the couple was a pastor in the same presbytery David was a pastor in. He'd also been at David's ordination years earlier, just by chance. The Black member of the couple was incredibly fit and well adjusted, so he was basically *my* twin. David told me about this other couple, Tony and Dan, and how similar they were to us, and I replied, "Oh, wonderful, let's make them our nemeses!"

I had nothing against these strangers, of course. And I had spent so much time trying so hard to make friends. But they seemed so similar to us on paper, and I was so out of practice, that I just skipped a step from casual acquaintance and went straight to rivals. Plus, it seemed like a great opportunity. I mean, who doesn't want to form internecine rivalries that can power us through the next few decades of our lives, inspiring us to greater achievement? Think of how the space race motivated American innovation. You like Velcro? This is how you get Velcro! The world is built on rivalry. Would it have been easier if Russia and America had just collaborated, friendly-like? Sure, I guess. I mean, obviously. But are we really built for friendship? Shakespeare had Marlowe, Mozart had Salieri, Bette Midler and Lily Tomlin in *Big Business* had Bette Midler and Lily Tomlin in *Big Business*. And David and I had the *other*, more established local interracial gay couple, who were religion-adjacent. Soon I would be invincible.

Unfortunately, the world was robbed of the true extent of my achievements because David reminded me that we were not trying to make Velcro, we were trying to make friends. I'm not as good at making friends, mostly because I insist on inserting references to Salieri into casual conversation and calling white couples same-sames. And in Baltimore I was feeling squirrelly, insecure, and these feelings posed something of an obstacle to the pursuit of a wide circle of close friends. But I dared to hope that, perhaps buoyed by David's less deranged demeanor, we could succeed where we'd failed at the first apartment building. Perhaps we could make . . . what's the word? Friends.

And then eventually turn them into rivals. Just throwing an idea out there.

We started to hang out with Tony and Dan. They had us over for dinner and we brought wine; we had them over for dinner and they brought wine; we looked at their bathroom remodel admiringly. This is adult friendship—trading a bottle of Beaujolais back and forth and commenting on grout. Sometimes we'd hang out one-on-one, mixie-matchie, like friends do! It was lovely and a wonderful turn of events after the disorientation of our first year and the clerestory apartment. I enjoyed their company so much that when they mentioned they went to the CrossFit gym down the street from me and invited me to come sometime, I responded, "This is all I've ever wanted!" And I actually went. This, too, is adult friendship—jumping on a box and struggling to do a pull-up at six in the morning for the company.

After we'd been in our new apartment in Remington for a few months, Tony and Dan bought a huge, gorgeous house.

I said, "David, this is an act of war."

He said, "I don't think you can take someone else's house personally."

You *absolutely* can take someone else's house personally, and I absolutely did on the many occasions they had us over for extraordinarily welcoming parties with great food amongst their many other equally welcoming friends. Their house was one of the three-story brick rowhomes in Baltimore that were mansions a hundred years ago. It had high ceilings and a grand staircase, which I dreamt of dramatically descending like Carlotta in *The Phantom of the Opera*. The floors went on forever, the former servants' quarters having been converted into more rooms. It was so much house, and they'd made it so warm and inviting. It reminded me, in size and architecture, of the house my parents lived in, the house where I grew up. And I felt the pangs of longing for the familiar. I had loved that house in my youth—the vastness, the structure. The abundance of physical space was a beautiful symbol in a world where so many other forces tell you that you deserve so little. That house, the people in it, the world my parents created, was a dream. It was only the world outside the windows—the effects of decades of bad policy and systemic oppression, the filming crew of *The Wire*, the lack of possibility—that made me unhappy. For so long I'd avoided Baltimore and all its trappings, and here I was, looking at this similar but not-so-similar couple living in a similar but not-so-similar house that I loved and thinking, *Maybe this place can be home again for me.* I could feel the life we wanted, a parallel-universe version of the life we had in Philly, getting closer. I was, often, happier.

I talked so much about Tony and Dan's gorgeous house that David asked me if I wanted to buy a house of our own, maybe near them. Finally, he'd converted to rivalry.

I told him, "That's very sweet, but I don't believe in home-ownership." He found this surprising. I found it surprising, too! Sometimes I just be saying stuff. But it was true that I didn't really *get* equity. David tried to explain it to me. I said, "That sounds like white nonsense."

Besides, I loved the apartment. I loved being so close to people. I loved casually running into neighbors and their pets in the elevator. I loved living two floors up from my doctor's office (and yet always being late). This was where we belonged.

By the Christmas of our second year in the new place, we'd felt emboldened enough by our slowly growing circle that we threw a small get-together in the apartment. Mary Richards behavior. I struggled for a week over how to write the invitation text, but we got there, folks!

Our lives were blooming. David and I had joined a gay kick-ball team that was starting up in March; I'd been made captain under duress, but I was excited about actually meeting the people we'd been assigned to play with. My book was coming out in a few months also, and I'd just gotten advance copies, which was thrilling and overwhelming. I felt on the precipice of something huge, a way of reaching people more closely than I ever had before. I was going to have book friends! I had started making little packages of glitter to give out at book-tour stops as themed souvenirs. My whole life was glitter. In February, I'd be going to a couple cities on the East Coast, and then in March and April I was going to the West Coast and the Midwest. I was particularly excited about stopping in Nashville at Parnassus Books, where I was going to buy Brian an Ann Patchett–themed tote bag and hopefully get her to sign it. This is how you win therapy.

I looked around at our Baltimore apartment full of people who were mostly strangers to us a year or two before, and I let myself feel hope. I'd made connections with the local theater company, and they were going to do a new play of mine that next year; the director came to the get-together and complimented our bookshelves, which is the highest honor I can think of. Another theater company had expressed interest in programming me the following season. I could feel the pull of rehearsal rooms and theaters full of people just around the corner. Things were turning around, little by little. Making friends as an adult may have been embarrassing, but *life* is embarrassing. And I loved life. I *could* be happy here. The new story for me was all just beginning.

The rest of this wonderful life awaited just past the holiday, in the glorious new year, 2020!

Part Two

HOMEGOING

Congratulations, The Best Is Over!

Here's an interlude from the future. I'm standing on the long driveway of a house in a suburban neighborhood so spread out it seems like the country. It's night; the only light comes from a lamp at the edge of the road. There is no one else around, no signs of life, and no noise. Post-apocalyptic vibes. Then: a clatter in the darkness. A deer steps into the pool of light from the streetlamp. It trots up the drive a bit and then catches sight of me. We both freeze and look at each other. If you're a character in a prestige cable drama, being stared at by a deer in an empty suburb or wooded area means you're about to go through some sort of massive personal change. I'm not really in the mood to go through a personal change right now. I say to the deer, "Do you have a message for me?"

The deer replies, "Huh?"

I say, "I've been watching *The Leftovers* on HBO and I thought . . . Never mind, it just seemed like you and I were supposed to have some kind of transformative experience together?"

The deer says, "You're not even supposed to be here!" And then it bolts into the darkness, racing at full speed down the center of the road.

I stay on the driveway until I can't hear its hooves against the asphalt anymore. Then I turn, walk through the yard, and let myself into a small farmhouse. This is where I live now.

Five months earlier, David and I were sitting on our couch in our second Baltimore apartment, across from our sideboard, which had recently been cleared of the vases and records that used to be on it so that it could serve as the backdrop for "Zoom church." It was late April, six weeks since the full force of the pandemic reached the United States. There was a pile of home-made masks sitting on the rack by the front door and, under-neath them, a box of the thick disposable shop towels that mechanics use to wipe up oil. While doom-scrolling at four one morning, I'd read a tweet that said you could put the towels inside fabric masks to approximate an N95 mask's filtration, which we all know now is not quite scientifically accurate but sure seemed like a good enough idea at the time.

On the sofa, David and I were buried in our phones, resting our eyes from a long day of staring at our laptops. We hadn't interacted with anyone else in person in weeks. I was scrolling through Facebook. I gasped and turned to David. "Did you know Mark and Evan bought a house?"

Mark and Evan were a couple we'd met through Tony and Dan, who were just as welcoming and friendly and well ad-justed, a counterpoint to me. We liked both of them so much. They'd had us over and we'd had them over and they'd been at the Christmas party, as well. We wanted to be their friends. And we thought it was quite possible. Anything was possible in 2020!

And one of those possibilities—a surprise to me—was that Mark and Evan had stopped renting in Baltimore City and pur-chased a home way out in the northern part of Baltimore County, an area that politically was a reddish shade of purple and stretched out into farmland. I scrolled through their post about their new house and their wishes for everyone to come over when all this was over.

"I didn't know they let gays live out there," I said to David, envy creeping into my voice.

I didn't want a house. I was happy in our apartment when it felt like an extension of a growing life, a place that filled up with friends at holidays or after work on random evenings. I didn't want a house. But the fact was, our friends had houses and I was starting to take it personally.

We scrolled through the Zillow listing for Mark and Evan's house, because that's what you do. You look at the features of friends' houses and decide if you'd make the same choice. You look at the price and remark, "Oh, that's smart, that's a good deal," or "Wow, that's pricey. Do you think they're rich?" You wonder, just a little, if this is reason enough to change your mind about what you want.

The next day, David sat next to me on the couch in front of the sideboard-turned-makeshift-altar. He handed his phone to me gingerly and said with a practiced casualness, "Just so you know, there's another house for sale near Mark and Evan. If you want to look."

Apparently, the key to getting me to consider the appeal of the suburbs is locking me in my city apartment for fifty-two days. On day fifty-three, suddenly I'm like, "You know what really rings my bells? A Nest camera, a cul-de-sac, and an HOA handbook full of microaggressions. Wisteria Lane, here I come!" I've made a big show in my life about how I am spiritually, mentally, and philosophically opposed to the suburbs. Not for political reasons, although I do think society functions better in closer proximity, but mostly because suburbs are terrifying to me. The suburbs are so often sold on how quiet they are and how much wooded area they're near. Now, what do I want with an endless expanse of dark, quiet woods? Who do I look like, the Blair Witch?

Despite all that, we toured the house. We and the realtor wore masks and stood at dueling distance from each other for safety. I wondered what the house smelled like. We went back to our apartment. I flinched every time I heard a neighbor coughing through the walls. We did Zoom church in our living room, David on camera, me running tech. We toured again. I didn't know what I was supposed to be looking for. I turned on the sink. It worked. Good enough for me. I eyed the woods beyond the back fence warily. David suggested that we could put lights on the fence so that I wouldn't be afraid. I suggested the kind of spotlights they use to summon Batman.

We weren't in a quarantine bubble with anyone, because David's job had too many opportunities for exposure, so I had to call my parents and tell them we were thinking about the house. They looked it up on Zillow. They said, "They let Black people live out there?"

We began to let ourselves imagine a life in that house. Being there felt like a respite from the claustrophobia of the apartment and the anxiety of the city. We walked in the yard. "The grass is so soft!" I called through my mask. We asked our realtor questions about the well that supplied the house with water, a feature I'd never encountered before. I was like, "You mean the thing that trapped Baby Jessica?!" Our realtor reassured me it was a good well. *It's true,* I thought. I had seen the water come out of the faucet. We put an offer in on the house. People negotiated over email. The offer was accepted. We bought the house. *This is too easy,* I thought. *What's the catch?*

Here's an interlude from the past. I am with my family at a crowded open house in Lutherville, Maryland, a suburb near the private school where my brothers went. I'm twelve or so. I can't tell why this house is so popular. It's not that big, and everything in the house seems a little old—the unpolished fixtures, the scuffed wooden doors, the cracked linoleum floors. Plus, the owner's belongings are everywhere, and the walls are covered with framed photos, documents, and, horrifyingly, dozens and dozens of taxidermic animals. I don't understand why people want this house, but, more important, I don't understand why I want this house. But I do, so badly.

My family is in a season of possibility. My parents are newly devoted to the idea of getting us out of our house in the city. More and more of the houses around us are losing renters and being abandoned by their negligent owners; the drug trade has picked up at the edges of the neighborhood. The dream that my parents were sold in the late seventies of a Black neighborhood on the cusp of revitalization despite decades of redlining hasn't come to fruition. It's seeming unlikely that it ever will. So they've found a new dream.

My mother tells me that she has a vision of me sitting in a backyard somewhere, under a huge tree, reading until the sun goes down. She wants that for me. And when she says it, I feel the dream grow around me, taking root underneath me, enveloping me in its shade. I want this for myself. We, as a family, dream of space and community, and safety, and a version of America rooted in possibility. And so we have started going to open houses.

We descend as one group into the finished basement at the open house. Afternoon sunlight mottled by dust is coming in through small windows near the ceiling, setting aglow white wood-paneled walls that are covered with bookshelves. The crowd moves and I'm able to get a closer look at the books. The owner seems to be very interested in World War II. And the Civil War. A history buff? There's something off about the collection, haunted. And then I look up—on the wall, in the space where a bust of a deer might go, is a shelf full of memorabilia. Nazi badges, Confederate money. A flag. We turn around; this is not our dream house.

There are what feels like an endless stream of open houses in this period. An endless stream of potential dreams. Our hopes rise, they fall. We stay in the city. One afternoon we go out to the house of a friend from church, a Black woman living in a Black suburb. Two doors up from her, there's a new house being built. They've just poured the foundation; it's little more than a hole in the ground. My family wanders down to look and, like magic, the dream rises up in front of us as walls and windows and rugs and tables and people.

"This is our house," my mother says.

She marches back to the barbecue at our church friend's house and starts telling people that we are going to buy the house that is just barely becoming at the end of the street. She takes a friend to show her the foundation of possibility. They walk around the perimeter. The friend comes back. "That is your house," the friend says.

My mother brings more people over to our house. They all walk around the base. She says she is doing a reverse Joshua, the Biblical figure who, in the Battle of Jericho, led the Israelites to march around the walls of the city. They circled Jericho every day for six days, and on the seventh day the walls of the city crumbled and the Israelites entered, triumphant. We're not trying to invade a city, and we want to raise walls, not tear them down, but still she marches. We march around the dream house seven times. It's set.

We leave the barbecue, jubilant.

I wait.

But something happens, I don't know what, and the dream house never becomes real. It's someone else's dream. We never get it even though my parents tried, even though we marched. Years will pass; we never leave the house in the city. But for all of my life I'll be thinking of the intense power of a shared dream on that summer afternoon. ·

Privately I'd wonder about the house that David found; *was* this our house? It was so far from the city and promised such a different experience of life. David had grown up in suburban houses and with more economic opportunity than I did; he didn't feel the same discomfort about it. He was excited, and I let that excitement guide me. I could see what was possible. But was it possible for me?

I didn't belong in the suburbs. I've never gotten up at seven in the morning to blow leaves with a gas-powered device that sounds like an F-16. I don't know what mulch is, and I don't want to learn. I'd heard that foxes scream in the night in the suburbs, and of all the creatures I've heard make a racket out in the street after dark, I do think a fox is the most terrifying. It's little and furtive and quick and red and now it's screaming at me? I'm calling an Uber and an exorcist. The suburbs have Paneras, but they also have beasties and homeowners associations, and I don't think the cost balances out.

If a homeowners association ever fixed their mouth to tell me what to do, I would lose my mind. I just don't ever see myself living under those kinds of dystopian conditions. You're going to tell me what I can and cannot do with this piece of private property that is owned by my close personal friend PNC Bank? You better get out of my face! It is bonkers to me that people will spend hundreds of thousands of dollars on a home and still have to go sit in front of a panel of petty bureaucrats in golf shirts to ask for permission to paint a mailbox. On your own land? Just the *thought* of an HOA makes me want to become an anarchist! Calling up Emma Goldman like, "Girl, you won't believe this, but they said I can't put in a pool!"

But on paper the house made sense, and there wasn't an HOA, and, way back in the past, David and I had sat at an Italian restaurant on our first date, and we shared a dream that seemed an awful lot like this house. We both talked on the date about how much we loved gatherings of family and friends, places where you could tell stories you've told a million times and stay far longer than you intended. I told him about how my parents hosted the Watch Night dinner after church service on New Year's Eve, and our house would fill with people and food and laughter in the wee small hours of a dawning year. He told me about how his aunt and uncle had a house with a big back-yard strung with tiki lights, where they threw elaborate parties at which his uncle would announce the start of the festivities by blowing into a conch shell. On our first date, through our stories, we shared a dream to have homes where friends and loved ones would congregate and convene.

In some ways, that shared dream of how rich and warm our lives could be has built the house of our relationship. It pulled us through isolation in apartments, and periods of depression where we felt we'd lost our ways, and the new, COVID-separated world. It beckoned us, it seemed, out to a half acre of land where David could plant raised beds of vegetables to eat and we could set out tables on the lawn for parties. We talked of putting an addition on the house, a dining room that was perpendicular to the main structure and ran along the path of the raised beds. The walls would be floor-to-ceiling windows and the roof would open up to skylights, and we'd have friends and family over to sit around a huge table bathed in summer light. And when nieces and nephews and godchildren visited, we'd turn the seating benches for the table into beds where they could sleep, their faces turned up to the open night sky as they created dreams of their own.

In abstraction, homeownership seems like a simple dream and one to which I was entitled. But I kept thinking about the complicated and sometimes fraught system I was buying into. Was it wrong to buy a house during this period when so many people had so little? Was it giving up to leave a city in favor of a suburb? Would making this purchase do anything to bring about the more just world of shared resources and less scarcity that we both wanted? Did I have the wrong dream? I judged myself even as we kept moving forward. But I need to paint the picture of what was going on in the larger world, because I wasn't just juggling the moral calculus inside. By this time, it had been months since anything felt normal. There were no masks yet available to buy, so we were all walking around with bandannas on our faces like gunslingers in the Wild West. On Etsy, I ordered a bedazzled mask with fringe hanging off the bottom, with plans to "wear it to a party someday." Unclear what I meant by this when I said it, but I have never worn that mask.

There was a *New York Times* article about people who believed they were quarantining with ghosts. And, you know what, good for them. All the restaurants were closed. TV had run out. There were no new episodes of anything. Reporters were filming the news from their living rooms. Every five minutes you saw a dog or a child wandering onto live TV. People were doing the weather report from their pantries. Celebrities were going live on Instagram just to talk, and, it turned out, many celebrities are incredibly boring! Meanwhile, one of the few non-boring celebrities, Cardi B, interviewed Bernie Sanders on Instagram while wearing a blue wig with Princess Leia buns. (Cardi was wearing the wig.) After that interview finished, she stayed on live, silently and elaborately ate a mango, wiped her hands, and then gave away one thousand dollars to a random fan. It was the most captivating hour of broadcast I have ever seen, and yet there wasn't a single moment of it that my brain understood.

The White House was holding COVID briefings where a rotating casts of flimflam men, Batman villains, performance artists, conspiracy theorists, future felons, and the haunted Victorian doll that is Jared Kushner would take turns lying to the American people, abdicating responsibility, and making ludicrous suggestions in the name of public health. Everything was so extraordinarily unhinged.

It had become clear to everyone by this point that we were in the middle of it, and we were on our own and we didn't quite know when the middle would end or what we were going to do to save ourselves. And the cheery, make-do bursts of creativity—Zoom game nights, celebrities singing "Imagine," making jokes about being on mute—suddenly became the rote, day-in-and-day-out facts of life. I spent hours of every day sitting on a tall kitchen chair in the study, with my laptop shoved onto a shelf in our hutch, staring at my own face in a Zoom window like I was both sides of a Marina Abramović performance. I looked tired.

The news was all bad. There was no pop culture, which is tough when you're writing a humor column about pop culture and politics. The air was stale. The streets were eerily quiet, though I read on Twitter that in New York, sirens were going twenty-four hours a day.

And in the midst of all of that, George Floyd was murdered and Breonna Taylor was murdered and video footage of the murder of Ahmaud Arbery came to light after a coordinated cover-up. And so much that bubbled constantly beneath the surface of everyday life in America rose up through the fraying edges and overtook us. Suddenly we were out in the streets in protest, only to be met with riot police and violence. The still quietness that hung heavy in the air of Baltimore City was soon jangled by the frantic drone of helicopters at all hours of the day and night. Activists started tearing down Confederate monuments all across the country again, igniting a new wave of hand-wringing punditry about history and decorum. But this was not a decorous time. In May, a white woman called the police on a Black man who was bird-watching in Central Park, setting off months of outrage. And at the end of that same week, Omar Jimenez, a Black reporter for CNN, was arrested live on the air while covering protests in Minneapolis. It struck me that the conversation around the bird-watcher and the reporter centered on how calm, presentable, and respectable they were. That was part of the shock: that Black men whose presence was so decorous could also find themselves under threat. But I wasn't shocked, of course. Because, as I wrote on *ELLE.com*, it doesn't matter if you're good. It doesn't matter how well you perform your worthiness. There is something in the root of America that will treat you as a threat.

I have never felt such vivid emotional darkness, even during the worst periods of depression. I felt the black absence of hope as a constant, an active thing, a space just in front of my face. I lived online. I died online. I saw it happening a hundred times a day on the newsfeed.

Something, everything, had broken open. And the same president who, at a fall 2020 debate, would tell a white supremacist group, "Stand back and stand by," leaned into the moment with an ambivalent shrug and an opportunistic glint in his eye. After months of pandemic delay, he resumed holding public rallies on Juneteenth—June 19, 2020—in Tulsa, Oklahoma, where ninety-nine years earlier a mob of white vigilantes had committed one of the worst massacres of Black lives in American history.

I don't want to tell you any more about how it was. You were there. And in the midst of all this, you got up in the morning and sometimes you'd wonder, "Is this what life is?" And then you'd cobble together the crumbs of your day and move on. It felt, societally and spiritually, apocalyptic. But it was not an apocalypse. The lights remained on. The taxes came due. Nothing began and nothing ended. It was a working apocalypse, like having a salad at your desk.

I felt severed from any world that I knew and from myself in that world. My humor-column output dribbled down to nothing because I found very little to be funny. That had never happened before. No matter what, I was able to work. But what the hell was I working toward? With a constant reminder that no matter my sense of self, there was only one story for me as a Black person in America, I withdrew more and more until there was nothing left but a hard, jagged stone of rage sitting in our apartment.

No dreams. Just dread.

So when David slid his phone to me with a photo of a small house with a huge backyard far up in the county, it appeared to me an open door out of this place that had bound me up. And all of my fears about suburbs and apprehensions about home equity and anxieties about money seemed so much smaller than the promise of a place where I could be safe, where I could step out of my door and stand on land that I pretended to own, under the sun, free.

When you do a Google Maps search of the house and use the walking feature to travel down the road a bit, the first thing you see is a house with a big Trump sign cattycorner to our house. I saw this on the first night that we looked at the Zillow listing. The image copyright on Google says that it was captured in November of 2016, which feels a bit on the nose, don't you think? I saw it and I thought, *Do you really believe that there's freedom in this place?* But the Trump house was across a supposedly busy road with no sidewalk on either side, and surely they'd taken the sign down in the last four years. Plus, the dream of buying your first home tells you that in doing so you are exerting control over your destiny and the destinies of those that come after you. In this space, it says, you can create the world you want to be in.

The house was built in 1935 and then remodeled in 1985 to add such luxuries as plumbing. It was modest, about 1,200 square feet, with three smallish bedrooms upstairs. You could always feel the ghost of what it used to be, although I could never imagine what other lives had happened in these little rooms with low ceilings.

But the land was the selling point. The house was surrounded by the natural world, sitting on a half acre that sloped down from a line of trees from which deer roamed with blithe abandon, hopping over the fence and munching on the hostas, carrying no news of the future. I had never had a reason to imagine what half of an acre was. It was so much land, a badonk of a backyard. We could do anything on it. We could build, we could plant, we could fill it with people. We could be happy. Here.

I thought about the legendary forty acres and a mule, the dangled promise of land and opportunity extended in front of formerly enslaved Black people, though never delivered upon. If nothing else, I was making progress. The dream plunged roots down into the earth and rose up around me with such incredible force that sometimes I had to stop where I stood until I got my bearings. One half of an acre. It was mine. Thirty-nine and a half more to go.

Jericho

I wanted to write a letter introducing David and myself to the new neighbors. As we prepared to move to the 'burbs, I vacillated between two trains of thought. On one hand, I was determined to approach this house and this neighborhood with openness. My desire was to commit to the community that I dreamt of. On the other hand, I was living in America in the summer of 2020, and I had few illusions about all the things that can happen when you show up somewhere you're not expected or not wanted.

The letter was an attempt to speak to both. It would be a way to put our faces to the address and to extend a friendly handshake in a time of social distance. It would also be a warning. I didn't know who lived in the other houses in this overwhelmingly white, rural-adjacent suburb, including the houses that still had Trump signs and the houses with huge, homemade Trump billboards, and the houses with even more politically extreme flags and signs. But I could make an educated guess. And in my more paranoid moments, I'd let myself put demographic details to those guesses and then intentions. It terrified me, at times, and so I decided to write to conquer that terror. The words of the letter would say, "We'd like to meet you when all this is over," but what it really would communicate was, "Please don't murder me when I stand in my yard; I promise you I should be here." The letter would read, "We hope you're safe and healthy." But between the lines it would whisper, "If you're going to burn down our house, do it now, before we move in." These were days when my thoughts turned even more often to Ahmaud Arbery, a Black man hunted and killed by three white men while jogging, and Botham Jean, a Black man who was killed in his own home by an off-duty police officer who claimed to mistake his apartment for hers.

I thought also of how many times I'd seen *A Raisin in the Sun* and how many times I'd joked—but not really joked—that the central Black family, the Youngers, should have taken the money that the racist white neighborhood offered them in exchange for not moving into the house that the Youngers bought. In my vision of their futures, the Youngers keep buying houses in white suburbs and keep getting paid off by racists until they are the richest people in Chicago.

I think this is a good logistical solution, and while maybe it doesn't feel like justice, it certainly feels like revenge, which is justice's second cousin on its father's side. But I never really have an answer for what the Youngers are supposed to do once they've amassed a fortune. At what point as a Black person in America do you have enough stuff—money, property, political capital—to stop being treated like a Black person in America? And how can that possibly be what you want, when all is said and done? What do you profit from losing yourself?

In the end, I didn't send the letter.

Once in the house, still quarantining, the only time I left was to pick up curbside groceries or to go to the hardware store. Some of the anxiety I felt being in such an unfamiliar place receded. We were making the house ours, putting up wallpaper and working on the garden, and it was easy to forget the mysteries of what happened behind our neighbors' doors, at least for a little while. Occasionally, I'd let myself go grocery shopping inside one of the two stores up the road from us in a more rural white town. These grocery stores were nice though they didn't offer curbside pickup, because the pandemic apparently wasn't happening there. But they were usually very empty and grocery shopping is one of my purest pleasures in life, so I'd treat myself.

I was in the self-checkout line, almost finished, when I glanced up at the magazine rack and saw, between a tabloid with Angelina Jolie on the cover and a fall-recipes magazine starring Rachael Ray, an entire magazine devoted to disaster prepping. The cover advertised articles on keeping your family safe, securing your valuables, navigating COVID-19, and—in the biggest, boldest letters—what to do about "civil unrest."

I had never seen anything like this before. It was like a *Reader's Digest* for survivalists and paramilitary hobbyists, with a soupçon of race panic. A *Prepper's Digest,* if you will. The cover model was a grimacing white man with a high-and-tight haircut and a bushy beard. His face was sooty, save for the outline of a pair of goggles, which now he had slung around his neck. He wore a black ribbed tank top over glistening muscles and a black leather jacket. And I know I'm describing something that might sound a little Tom of Finland, but in that suburban supermarket, next to Rachael Ray, this stern white man, standing in front of an explosion, was terrifying.

I had always felt that there were conversations that I was adjacent to but not privy to in these neighborhoods, and here was a whole digest of them! I looked around, sure someone was going to come over and tell me to keep my eyes on my own business. But no one was looking at me. My hand shot up to the magazine. I flipped it open to an article that offered "unique ideas for arming yourself." I slammed it shut. Do they sell this in your supermarket? You're just in there buying your Rice-a-Roni and your Charmin and you decide to also get a magazine that will break down the difference between castle doctrine and stand-your-ground.

It was like I'd stumbled upon a secret. A secret that I suspected kept getting Black people killed. I continued scanning my groceries and averted my eyes.

Then, right before I finished, I reached up, snatched the magazine, scanned it, and stuffed it in a bag under a loaf of bread. But I was so embarrassed about buying it and giving in to my ambient paranoia that I hid it from David under a box in the kitchen for months. I didn't want to talk about my fear. It takes effort to articulate, and I didn't have the energy. Plus, as much as I knew he'd understand, even share my fear, I didn't want to wrestle with the feeling that I was just doing America wrong. Life feels, sometimes, like I'm in a different world from some of the people around me, even my husband. It's a world that exists for all of us in plain sight but has clear boundaries for some. The double consciousness of a Black American experience has been well documented, but that doesn't always stop it from feeling like a Chicken Little situation. What does it mean if the sky is falling only on me?

And it wasn't about the racial makeup of the area or my assumptions about their politics. It wasn't about the Trump house or how many people on the Nextdoor app seamlessly went from complaining about masks to warning of suspicious brown people driving through neighborhoods. It was about the fear that I'd walked into a room where people were having a "just us" conversation and what they might do when they discovered

I'd been eavesdropping. I like to believe I can go anywhere in this country, but that belief comes with a big asterisk called history.

Almost every day I'd think, at least once in passing, about being killed by a police officer or a neighbor on our property. I thought of the myriad ways that things could be misunderstood. I thought about it and then I went on with my day, because there was nothing I could do about being Black and in my own home, living the American dream.

The quiet was too quiet. I found I couldn't sleep with the sound of nothingness at the house. You ever sleep in blissful, empty silence? It's atrocious. Plus, every little noise would startle me—the house creaking, an animal moving through the yard, a voice carrying from a neighboring property.

I don't trust the isolation, the stillness, the empty expanse. I'm a city mouse. I need the racket. I come from sirens and a recorded voice shouting "hello!" from ice cream trucks. I come from grid systems and corner stores. I come from farmers markets in random parking lots and herb gardens in teeny tiny cement backyards. I come from protected bike lanes and people sitting on the front stoop. I don't romanticize the city; I have experienced the harsh edge of city living enough times to know that no place is perfect but not enough times to make me a cable news commentator whose beat is "racially coded comments about lawlessness." A city is a promise to society that is broken more times than it's upheld. But it's a promise I believe in with all my heart.

Most of the time, however, the benefits of the house in the suburbs brightly outshone my anxieties. The supermarkets were well stocked. Packages could sit on your porch all day, undisturbed. Our neighbors on our side of the street were wonderful, and we'd sometimes yell like-minded conversations about the upcoming election over the fence. The election was all anyone could talk about. Trumpism was escalating in dangerous ways; the anxiety over the possibility of political violence or upheaval was unbearable. We chattered about it amiably in the backyard, like we were exchanging recipes for pound cake.

I went weeks without hearing a helicopter in the new house, but, interestingly, one of the primary negative aspects of city life—the sound of people shooting guns in the night—still happened out in the 'burbs. I presumed they were coming from hunters, but, baby, a gunshot is a gunshot. The suburbs are ghetto, too.

In my sleeplessness, I became a night watchman, sitting at the window, staring at the road and the darkness. Cars would sometimes pull into our driveway and turn around to go the other direction on the two-lane road by the house. If this were a city, the noise wouldn't have even woken me and, if it had, I wouldn't have thought anything of a car turning, or even stopping, outside the house. But this silent, isolated neighborhood was different. I'd sit up at night, squinting at the few cars that drove by, muttering, "Don't you slow down. I don't have time for a climactic battle today."

The trash truck came at 2 A.M. in the neighborhood. Ask me how I know. Because in the silence, it rumbled down the street and caused such a clatter, I ran to the window to see what was the matter! The first time it happened, I sat bolt upright in bed, sure this was the militia or something come a-calling. When I saw that it was just a municipal service, my first thought was, *I need to get on the Nextdoor app and talk about this! This is outrageous!*

Oh, how quickly we forget ourselves.

After a few weeks of waking at the slightest noise, I was finally able to settle in a bit and reach a REM cycle or two. The trash truck still roused me, but for the most part I was able to sleep through the night, no longer being driven to madness by the crunch of a deer's hoof on a leaf three houses down. And it was during one of these nights that a call from my mother came through at one in the morning. I was again immediately wide awake, because a middle-of-the-night phone call is a fearsome thing. I could barely hear her—the house did not get cellphone reception, and you could only make calls over Wi-Fi—but the distress in her voice came through clearly. I started to panic. She was outside their house in the city; someone had run into both of their cars, totaling them, and then fled the scene, leaving the car behind. She was waiting for the police, but she'd locked herself outside. My father was inside; he couldn't get down to her because he was recovering from an injury. As I listened, I started to scramble into my clothes, careful not to wander into the Wi-Fi dead zones that I'd already learned would cut our phone call off. She needed my help, she said. I told her I was on my way.

"Hello?!" she called, the panic rising in her voice. "Hello?!" And then the line went dead.

I tried to call her back and it went to voicemail. I tried again. I threw on a hoodie and went racing down the stairs, picturing my mother standing on the side of a street in downtown Baltimore all by herself. It was a thirty-minute drive and I cursed myself for taking myself so far away. My parents were by no means helpless, but I felt I'd failed them by following the allure of a yard and the night sky and some version of freedom I still hadn't worked out. I jumped into my car and sped past the Trump house. It was the first time I'd driven from our home in the dark. I had no reason to go out at night; there was nowhere to go. I turned on my high beams. Glowing eyeballs stared back at me from the sides of the road. Where in the world was I and why?

I kept trying my mother's phone, but I knew that I'd have to drive seven minutes before I got cellphone service again. I'd timed it. What was the plan for protection, I wondered, if something went wrong in our house and the Wi-Fi was out? What was my recourse if that nameless thing I feared came true? But then again, who was I going to call? The cops?

After seven minutes, I tried to reach her again. She sounded calmer. The police had arrived, and my youngest brother, Jeffrey, was on his way, too. She was not alone. I realized that taking these pitch-black country-road curves at Indy 500 speeds was not the look for me, and I slowed a little. "I'll be there soon," I said.

I got to my parents' block around 2 A.M. There are tall brick rowhomes like my parents' on one side of the street and, on the other, the burnt-out or collapsed shells of former homes. I parked on the burnt-out side, way up the street, behind a line of cars. I put on a mask and went charging down the center of the street, toward the intersection. Beyond the crosswalk I could see my mother, standing under lamplight by the wreckage of her car, taking photos. Jeffrey was with her, taking photos of my dad's car. In the middle of the street was the car that the driver had abandoned, the door still open. Next to it, a random man who looked like a bystander was just kind of hovering, shifting back and forth on the balls of his feet. His body seemed like it was dangling rather than standing, like he was a trench coat on a hanger. And in front of all this, half-turned away, was a police officer, a young woman with a brown ponytail.

My arms tingled from the adrenaline still coursing through me and I barreled through the intersection without looking, despite the obvious danger of drunk drivers and speeding cars.

I stepped through the crosswalk, and I came into the officer's line of sight. We were about twelve feet from each other. I saw her head turn toward me. I looked beyond her to my mother and then back at her. I kept walking. I noticed her arm move. Then her hand. She wrapped her fingers around her holstered gun.

I froze.

Oh, Eric, you've forgotten yourself.

All of the adrenaline drained out of my body at once, and it was replaced by a cold, bare terror. A plain thing. Not a panic, not messy. A calculation made from fear. I raised my eyebrows in a smile behind my mask. I checked the position of my hands. At my sides, limp, away from my pockets and my hoodie. Suddenly I dropped back into reality, what year it was, what neighborhood this was, who I was. I didn't move. Seconds earlier, my thoughts swirled with stress, worry, and questions, and now everything zeroed in on this one interaction and my ability to perform belonging, of all things, back in the broken-down shell of the redlined neighborhood where I grew up.

Still unmoving, I called cautiously to my mother, "Hi."

"Hi," my mother called back.

We kept our eyes on each other.

The police officer shifted her hand off her gun.

———

I've thought a lot about what possessed me to go speed-walking down a dark street in the direction of a police officer in the middle of Baltimore. As foolish as it was, I wasn't thinking about the cop at all. I was thinking about my mother; I was thinking about my father in the house. I was trying to piece together who the random man was—apparently, he'd been sent by the driver to retrieve the car. He actually asked the cop if he could take it when she was done with her report. Obviously, she declined.

I was in a different world when I got out of my car, that much was clear.

But the minute she put her hand on her gun, one question crystallized in my mind: *How afraid is this police officer of me?* Because that's all that mattered. That's all that separated me from the rest of my life.

Perhaps she wanted me to see the gesture. Perhaps we were having a conversation. I don't know. I never exchanged any words with her. All I know is what I saw—the tiny shift in her arm, the hand, her face. I had walked into a space where I was not expected. And that's all I needed to see to know what could happen between us and how I needed to proceed. I may have forgotten myself, but I remembered that I was in America.

After an hour or so, I drove back to my home in the dark.

Hostas Negotiator

The first time one of our next-door neighbors spotted David and me in the yard, she texted her husband, "I think the new neighbors are gay!" She added the two-men emoji to underscore the point. This was good news, she later told David. Her husband agreed. They were nervous about who would move in, having been friends with the single straight man who lived in the house before. You don't want noisy neighbors; you don't want jerks with bad opinions. So they were really excited about having the complete opposite: an emoji of two men.

They told us that, years ago, the house on the other side of them was owned by a gay couple they really liked. That gay couple had a pool, and our neighbors remembered them fondly as being a total blast. *Oh great,* I thought, *now we have to be interesting.* Our straight neighbors told David that one half of the gay couple was older and one was in his twenties. *Oh great,* I thought, *now we have to be Michael Douglas and Matt Damon in the Liberace movie,* Behind the Candelabra.

The neighbors, their fun gay neighbors, and the single straight guy who owned our house had all been friends. Once, they'd all gone over to the straight guy's yard, which at that time was just a muddy pit he let his dogs run around in. The gay couple was scandalized by the decrepit state of things and read him for filth for it. As a result, the straight guy had quickly hired someone to put in the hosta beds around the perimeter, a slate path, and ivy bushes around what was now our back porch.

This is what they dreamed of at Stonewall: One day a couple of wealthy May–December gays will so thoroughly bully a straight man that he'll spend thousands of dollars on landscaping. Yes, we can!

By the time we moved in, the slate path had mysteriously disappeared, but the landscaping around the porches remained and was in relatively decent shape, if overrun by Creeping Jenny. The rest of the yard had just been given over to grass and, when it rained even the slightest bit, a deluge of mud. Neither David nor I was keen on lawns. He for environmental reasons—they use a lot of water and don't give much back to the land. Me because I'm not trying to be out there mowing every Saturday morning in a worn white Hanes undershirt. So we devised a plan to turn it into a garden. We may not have been Liberace and Matt Damon, but we still had strong landscaping opinions and the desire to bully a heterosexual with them.

We saw the space around the house as a blank canvas of opportunity that had been left to weeds and mud. Everything was possible. David envisioned raised beds for herbs and vegetables, saplings, a pollinator garden, a moon garden around a fire pit, fruit bushes along the fence, a watermelon patch, and sunflowers at the crest of the hill. I saw the grade of the hill in the backyard and the way it seemed far too big for simple hobbying and thought, *Oh, we should make this an outdoor theater.* This is what's wrong with theater artists, frankly. We see literally any space with good sight lines and we think, *How wonderful it would be to do dramatics here!* What's the plan after that, folks? Start a theater company? Register as a 501(c)(3)? Solicit donations for a silent auction to benefit the capital campaign?

Looking back, perhaps this is where things went awry. David had a coherent plan for terraforming this yard, and I had a quixotic dream about turning it into a nonprofit arts organization. But that's marriage, right? Next time you meet a gay couple, be sure to ask them, "Which one of you is the Johnny Appleseed and which one of you is the famed acting teacher Konstantin Stanislavski?"

Anyway, we went with his plan.

Now, technically speaking, I've never had a yard. My parents have what the majority of city rowhome dwellers have behind the house: a little patch of grass, a cement square, and a three-story fire escape my brothers and I used to throw *Star Trek* action figures off of. (This last part may not apply to all city dwellers.) But with David, I shared that dream of a space for gathering. Out of the wreckage of the present, out of the rocky soil of our first few years in Baltimore, out of the lonely days we'd both experienced in the past: a yard full of life.

David was adept at gardening and farming, so I figured it would be easy enough to till, amend the soil, fix drainage issues, and finally plant on the half acre of land. Adam and Eve tended to the whole garden of Eden, and they didn't even have helpful YouTube videos to guide them. They literally showed up on earth like, "Sure, I can do whatever it is y'all do here." How hard could it be?

We ordered seeds, and tools, and vining plants, and raised beds, and materials for two huge compost bins so that we could reduce our waste and help feed the garden. We took near-daily trips to Lowe's to get electric tillers and soil amendments and many pairs of gloves because I kept losing mine. Whereas before our expenses had been books and succulents and takeout, now we were budgeting for tarps and shovels and other items in the So You Need to Bury a Body collection.

I spend a fair amount of my life on Instagram watching the exploits of gay couples who do home and garden improvement, and I was fairly certain we weren't like them, considering that I had never once filmed an Instagram of me doing anything related to any kind of improvement. One time I spotted a butterfly in the yard and, while filming it, improvised an interview between it and myself. I posted that to Instagram and people seemed to like it, but I wasn't sure I could turn that into a media empire. Still, I wondered if we could reinvent ourselves as individuals and as a couple once again.

Part of this stemmed from the *need* to reinvent. The pandemic was changing us. David's job required a near top-down rethinking; everything had to be rebuilt, reconceived, reorganized, from the way he did church to the needs of the congregation to what he was using the empty building for. It was draining and sometimes demoralizing, and at that time there was no end in sight. I had started thinking seriously about leaving *ELLE.com*, not for any dissatisfaction with the site but because I had lost track of the part of me that I felt made me good at writing the column. As much as it was built on snark and archness, for years I was able to write from a place of hope. If I'm not heading toward a place where I can feel joy, then hope in the present has nothing to hold on to.

To be reductive about it, at that time the present wasn't very fun. The news was so strange. The future was hazy. I struggled to find the punch line. Years earlier, I wrote a play where a playwright and a stand-up comedian have a long, contentious conversation about their shared past. It sounds autobiographical but, honestly, I do have original thoughts. The stand-up comedian says that she's pivoting to storytelling because jokes are about a problem, whereas stories end with solutions, or, if not solutions, resolutions. "Comedy is purgatory," she declares.

You tell the same joke over and over again; you never get out of the problem. I don't share that opinion, but there was something purgatorial about the work, the news, the new rhythm of life, the long, long middle.

The yard was part of that middle, too. An overwhelming place of constant becoming. You never really finish with a garden, I guess. But there was a part of me that wanted to try, if only to get to the end of the story. I saw it as a chance for us to make something, a way to externalize growth, and beauty, and nourishment.

But before all that, we had to dig a lot of holes.

We wanted to plant blueberry, marionberry, and blackberry bushes along the fence, so we started by digging three six-foot-long, two-foot-deep trenches, amending the soil, and finally planting the bushes, plus two hydrangeas and a St. John's wort that I'd found on the sale table at Lowe's. A little later we found twenty heather shrubs that were on their last legs and significantly reduced in price, so we bought and planted them, too. I am powerless against a bargain, even if it means I will have to do labor.

The ground by the fence was the hardest and most claylike. As we dug, my body started to complain, because it had never been asked to do anything like this in its life. My scar from my freak water-glass injury would throb as I gripped the handle, and my back shouted curses at me when I bent to scoop dirt out. My hands ached, my elbows burned, my knees got stiff and sore. I ordered a lower-back brace and carpal tunnel gloves. I bought stock in Tiger Balm. You know, there's a reason that Rose Royce sang in the song "Car Wash," "You might not ever get rich/But let me tell ya it's better than diggin' a ditch." Digging a ditch is famously the worst thing a person can do with their time and to their body.

I do feel that, culturally, we're kind of muddled in our thinking about ditches. Rose Royce's claims aside, most of pop culture says it's no big deal. For instance, when someone digs a ditch on TV, it is not at all like the experience I was having. Think of how many times you've seen a fictional character hastily dig a grave after killing someone. This happens all the time! People are constantly DIY'ing murder cover-ups! And when they do, are they dripping with sweat and having an asthma attack afterward? No! Do they have to stop every couple of minutes to do some back stretches they saw on a video called "Aging Bodies Are Agile Bodies"? They do not! And yet when I dig a one-foot hole, I, unfortunately, pass away. Now we need two ditches.

It's for these reasons that I believe I am not cut out for a life of crime. And worse yet, I am also not cut out for a life of putting bushes in the ground, which is a real pity, because that's exactly what I wanted to do to move forward.

Finishing the house became my obsession. The more progress we made, the more I was able to see what else needed to be done. With our garden, there was always more digging to do, more soil to amend, and, worst of all, weeds—everywhere, all the time, growing like . . . well, growing like weeds.

David found solace in gardening. He would sit out in the morning with coffee and watch the birds hunt for worms in our newly turned soil, then he'd grab a shovel and head out to another part of this ever-expanding project. He'd started ordering bulbs to plant for the following year and making plans to dig a pond midway up the yard. He was so good at the garden, and I loved to see it. But I was starting to resent the whole endeavor. My body hurt more and more. I didn't feel like I was actually good at any of the things I was doing. The garden, this dream space of community and creation, became the space where I felt loneliest.

After a while, we weren't working together much. With us in separate parts of the garden—or, more often, with him in the garden and me in the house—the new home was quiet. And it wasn't the garden's fault, of course. The outside world brought fresh horrors every day. Still, the question remained in my mind: How could two people who handled catastrophe, injury, and stress by shout-enunciating and external processing suddenly find themselves with so little to say?

The one place that I felt something like success was, ironically, the area where the straight guy who lived in the house before had failed. I noticed that there were three large, square pieces of slate near the hostas at the back porch and surmised that they must have been all that was left from the landscaping he'd been bullied into doing. I thought I could use them to make a little path from the back fence to the door.

I can't stress enough how little thought I put into how this slate-path thing was going to work. Even though they were incredibly heavy, I figured I'd dig them up and put them down somewhere else, and the grass and weeds would just respect the hierarchy of nature and leave them alone. So I dug up the slate and I wrangled it into a pile by the porch.

When I sank the shovel into the ground next to the last piece of slate, it made a sharp *thunk* and refused to go any lower. I got on my knees, dug into the dirt with my hands, and discovered another piece of slate beside it under a few inches of soil. So now I had four. I stabbed my shovel into another spot in the mud around the bed of hostas and found yet another large piece of buried slate. I was like Indiana Jones in *The Last Crusade*—the path was appearing before me.

As summer slipped into fall, I spent days jamming a shovel into random spots in the yard, waiting for that *thunk*, and then using a crowbar to hoist up another piece of slate. By the end I'd discovered twenty-seven pieces, the largest of which was over three feet long and two feet across. What was this straight man doing?! My dude bought Stonehenge and then was like, "Let the earth take it!" I wanted to call up the old neighbor Liberace and tell him, "You didn't bully that guy enough."

I knew I needed to address the erosion issues that buried the slate in the first place. I do not know where this knowledge came from. I have never thought once about erosion, and I certainly don't have any solutions for it stored away in my mind palace. I decided I would dig out the whole path from the step to the gate. I'd go down about two feet and fill the path in with materials that would absorb water, support the slate, and repel weeds, before I placed the slate. Yes, that's right—I am now a structural engineer. Hire me to make Stonehenge 2.

If I'd thought the whole plan through from the beginning, I'm sure I wouldn't have done any of this. None of this is in my nature. I have absolutely no knowledge of the tectonic integrity of a yard, or whatever, and I was overwhelmed by the immensity of so many other garden projects. But because it had started so simply and one thing had led to the next, I possessed a confidence that was perhaps misguided but certainly felt good. The path was coming together little by little, and I kept going. It's amazing what you come to believe is possible after ripping a seventy-five-pound rock out of the ground with your bare hands.

I dug the trench for the new path; I carted wheelbarrows full of dirt to the area of our land beyond the back gate; I made constant trips to Lowe's for gravel and sand that would take years to fully remove from the crevices of my little hybrid car. I pulled weeds and dreamt of flowers to replace them. I was never not dirty.

I redid the path, I added more wood chips, I filled in crevices with sand. I dumped water on top of the sand to see whether it would get absorbed. I did this for a month and then, at last, I was satisfied with the drainage. I lugged tons of slate into formation by hand, little by little, and filled in the spaces between the large pieces with more gravel. I lined the edges with the smooth, round stones I'd found, presumably another result of the last gay couple's bullying. I stepped across the path, as careful as Indiana Jones was. It held my weight. I had created a path to our home out of nothing! It took weeks of hard work in the sun; it was aching muscles and callused hands; it was grueling and it was lonely. But I'd finished it.

I felt a sense of accomplishment in a way that I never had before: to make something, not to prove your worth or your work ethic but just to add a piece of yourself to the space that we're in for such a short time. I stood on the path and watched David as he mapped out the place where he planned to dig a pond the following spring. He measured the area with his feet and planted little flags on the perimeter. I saw, for just a moment, where he was in his story. I saw the garden that could become, yes, but I also saw the garden as it was, the honoring of our own efforts, the time we'd chosen to spend individually creating. Oh God, was this mindfulness?!

I asked David what he got out of gardening. He said it cleared his mind of the myriad worries, logistical concerns, and anxieties that plagued him constantly with the new nature of his job. The garden starts in your head, he told me. It's the organization of space, it's potential, it's knowing how plants work with each other and how those plants respond to the conditions around them. It's thinking about the position of the sun in the sky and the temperature of the earth. It's considering where the planet is in space and where we are on the planet. It's creation. It's science. It's work and it's magic. For him it was a personal, spiritual practice.

We had separate work to do still, but I understood the need for the process, the space, the effort, in a way I hadn't before. The path wouldn't simply appear; I'd have to rip it out of the mud. So be it. Standing on ground that I'd formed myself, I felt powerful and also overwhelmed and also capable of bullying a straight man about erosion. And maybe, just maybe, when David and I found our way to each other in the middle of the yard, we could pursue my dream, too: starting a gay home-improvement Instagram account.

Determined to Enjoy Myself

I am absolutely not a survivalist by any means, but just before Election Night 2020, I did make a tiny gesture toward continued existence. I had enough misgivings about our neighborhood and the ever more rage-filled country as a whole to fear that something was going to go sideways. The tenor of the political environment had gotten frenetic; leaders and TV hosts were unabashedly spreading conspiracy theories, spouting white-nationalist talking points, and flirting with fascism. David, through his church work, was being invited to civil-disobedience trainings, one of which included recommendations on which gas mask to buy. Just a bunch of pastors looking at a Wirecutter article called "The Best Gas Masks for Being Attacked by Riot Police."

He and I talked in very general terms about what might be helpful to have around the house in various emergency situations, and then I did what I do best in a crisis: I went shopping. I thought, *Oh gosh, a gas mask is so extreme.* So instead I stopped in a bank and withdrew one thousand dollars. The teller was like, "Going somewhere?" and I was like, "No! Who said that? I'm not doing anything. Don't alert the marauders." I casually dashed out the door, put the envelope of cash in my glove compartment like a mobster, and thought about how wonderful it is to participate in democratic processes.

David and I had also conferred about home security. I am spiritually opposed to any doorbell cameras that upload footage to a cloud, because I don't know who is in that cloud. I'm not trying to aid and abet any robot or sinister company. Unless that cloud is the one that led the Israelites across the desert, I don't want anything to do with it. In retrospect, it may have been enough to have deadbolts in our neighborhood, considering that when David and I both locked ourselves out of the house in the same week, our friends who lived nearby were shocked to hear that we locked our doors at all. I grew up in downtown Baltimore on the set of *The Wire*, honey; you are never going to find me behind an open door like I'm a prize on *Let's Make a Deal*. Even my casket is going to have one of those little chain locks. Getting to heaven and opening the casket door just a crack. Looking at Saint Peter like, "Yes? Can I help you?"

In addition to the locks on the doors, David and I agreed that it might be helpful—if even just for our peace of mind—to have a couple more flashlights and a couple of baseball bats. Now, what I was going to do with a bat against some red-hat-wearing invader when I'm the same guy who was graciously invited not to play on the gay softball league after my first year, I don't know. That was Future Eric's problem. Present Eric's problem was, *And just where do I get a bat?*

I really thought hard about this. One of the promises of the suburbs is that you can get anything you want, but mostly what I wanted in those quarantined times was a Panera blueberry muffin or a suspiciously large amount of money from a joint savings account. A bat? In November? Eventually I remembered the existence of Dick's Sporting Goods store. You would not believe how expensive bats are! A simple wooden bat like I'm going as *Field of Dreams* for Halloween cost me forty-five dollars! Each! I was like, "Mr. Dick! I am just trying to survive white nationalism. Is there a discount? Please!"

My last stop was Lowe's, to get flashlights. By this time I had fully worked myself up into a tizzy of anxiety and, after spending an entire day trying to act casual while buying—yes, I must admit it—survival supplies, my façade was starting to slip. I got a cart at Lowe's and went up and down a few aisles like I was just browsing. Maybe I'll re-do my backsplash! Who knows? No one was paying me any mind at all, but I still felt like my presence all day had been a flashing warning light: This Black man thinks something is up! I do not under any circumstances want anyone to know I think something is up.

I passed through the flashlight aisle. "The generator is on the fritz!" I said aloud to absolutely no one. I grabbed two flashlights and a couple of lanterns. I turned a corner and went down another aisle, trying to make my way to the batteries and the checkout. Before I got there, however, I passed through a section of tools for clearing brush and chopping wood. Saws and clippers and axes. We don't believe in having guns in the house, but an axe? An axe seemed reasonable! Red Riding Hood vibes! I put the axe in my cart for self-defense against insurrectionists and wolves posing as grandparents.

I had sailed through the realm of preparation, loosed from the bounds of reasonable threat assessment, and was floating into the deep space of vengeance. If someone from the Whiteness Protection Program came into our house on Election Night, I was going to go Liam Neeson on them. As the founders intended.

I worried that I would have to come up with a story to explain the purchase to the cashier, but when I got to the counter, I saw that the cashier was Black. I thought we might have a moment of bonding, but she didn't care what I was buying at all. Even better!

What I love about David is that when I pulled up to the house and tumbled inside carrying two bats, a bunch of flashlights, a thousand dollars, and an axe, he said, "Thank you; now we're ready."

A couple of days later, after the election results were *finally* and peacefully decided, the country looked different for a moment. I took another day trip to Baltimore, with a different but equally peripatetic agenda. I was set to leave *ELLE* in December, with the intention of exploring work in TV and writing more books. I'd dedicated the early months of 2021 to working on a young-adult novel about queer Black teenagers who go on a *Ferris Bueller's Day Off*–style adventure in contemporary Baltimore. So I drove down to the city to refamiliarize myself and take notes on location details, as best I could with many businesses shuttered for quarantining.

I was excited about the opportunity for a field trip and the chance to tell this story. I was interested in writing about platonic love as one of the first ways that we learn about love, and I wanted an opportunity to craft a Black narrative, a queer narrative, and a Baltimore narrative that wasn't about trauma and making these two kids live through it in the name of plot momentum. Often, it feels like so many of us who are considered "other" don't have narrative or political value beyond the worst parts of our lives. But I know that we are more than that. I know that we can choose to share what is hard or choose to share some piece of our joy and hope, and the work is worthy either way.

The boys have a list of places that they go, and I followed essentially the same itinerary as I drove around in my car— a public pool, now shuttered and under reconstruction; the street where the Pride festival happens; a grand old mansion that in the world of the book houses a glorious after-party. I took pictures with my phone of empty streets and a hole in the ground next to an architect's drawing of a bustling pool. As I drove, other parts of the city that I hadn't envisioned in the book started jumping out to me. I spent half an hour photographing intricate graffiti murals around the corner from the place where the climax of the book happens. I passed by the public market where my father had worked for the last two decades and tried to capture the Times Square–like magic of the neon signage. I drove down Pennsylvania Avenue, snapping a picture of a marquee commemorating the Royal Theatre, the place where every significant Black artist from the twenties to the fifties played. I turned and drove down my parents' block. Across the street from their house, the abandoned and burnt-out buildings that had stood like haunted houses for years were being torn down by the city. In their place, they were planting a field of indigo that Maryland Institute College of Art students were going to use to dye textiles.

The book opens with the two boys hanging out in a cemetery, so I went there and took photos of intricately carved gravestones against a brilliant blue sky. As I raised my phone, I felt another Baltimore ghost watching from somewhere nearby: the person I was when we'd first moved back. This was a person who had felt alone driving through these streets even when the streets were crowded, a person who'd gone to another cemetery desperate for hope. But I was telling a different story now. A story about life.

At the end of the day, I took a final photo from the highest point in the hilly burial ground. You can see all the way downtown, past my parents' house, through the harbor, into the horizon. It was stunning, a city of beauty and public art and nature and food and possibility and character. And hope. Oh, how I missed it now. Baltimore. The greatest city in America.

Two months later, I was deep into writing the opening scene of the book when my brother Jeffrey texted the family group chat something like, "Stand by; I will let you know if/when I'm coming to get you." It was the afternoon of January 6, 2021. I knew what this was about. I read the text and then looked around the room—I was in my home office at the time—and thought, *Should I pack an overnight bag for the end of democracy?* I pulled a copy of *The Pelican Brief* off the shelf and put it on the desk. Good to have some light reading in exile. Exhausted from the effort, I texted back a thumbs-up, then sat back down in front of my laptop. I clicked away from my manuscript and scrolled through Twitter, watching people ransack the Capitol as I waited to potentially be retrieved. One tweet played a video of a member of Trump's inner circle at the previous year's Republican National Convention. She held her arms above her head like a movie villain and intoned apocalyptically, "THE BEST! IS YET! TO COME!" I thought, *I don't know about all that, sis.*

I wasn't expecting Jeffrey's text, but I wasn't surprised. Baltimore is forty-five minutes from D.C., which usually means that you've been to every Smithsonian on a field trip but every once in a while means that you think, *Hmm, if things go sideways, I fear I may be on the front row of history. Well, not the front row, but the mezzanine at least.* It was very in character for Jeffery to have an escape plan if things went even more sour than they were going (which, as we all know, was very likely and very much the objective from the jump). Jeffrey always has a plan. He works in cybersecurity and has become the chief problem-solver in our family. He is your middle-of-the-night phone call. Meanwhile, I'd just made myself a cup of tea, was searching for the right metaphor for my book, and had a load of laundry in. I did not have a plan and I was not prepared to flee.

It had been telegraphed for a few weeks that some rapscallions were going to descend upon Washington on the day that the electoral vote was to be ratified and start a-hootin' and a-hollerin'. And a-here they were. It wasn't a shock to see the videos of them online initially, but as they started to climb over walls and break into federal buildings, I did think to myself, *Well, this can't be right.*

Meanwhile, across town, David was at work preparing for Epiphany. He didn't have his phone with him that day, so he was in for quite a surprise when he got back in the car and turned on NPR, where they were broadcasting the worst news you've ever heard in the most relaxing dulcet tones. It's what we in the business call ASMR SOS. But, even without seeing Jeffrey's text, I already knew David likely had his go bag packed and waiting by the door. I appreciate this about David, like I appreciate this about Jeffrey. David's Eagle Scout training matches up very well with my brother's clear-eyed approach to protecting those he cares about. They both believe in survival. David and Jeffrey have talked about the Plan multiple times before, in ambiguous terms. Well, it was ambiguous to me, at least, because I always use those times as an opportunity to get a little snack from the kitchen. They'll be discussing different ways to reach some cabin in some mountain range, and meanwhile I'm like, "I found a *New York Times* recipe for a plum tart that I'm trying to perfect, so my schedule is pretty full right now." They aren't Preppers per se. They are prepared.

I am not. Look, I'm not irresponsible. I manage our finances, I monitor the 401(k), I downloaded a kit from the internet called "So You Wanna Write a Will." I am prepared for the best; I am prepared for the not-so-great. I am prepared for the inevitable. However, I refuse to prepare in any way for the worst.

I don't want to go to a cabin in the mountains! And then what? Forage? Well, first of all, at the time I was on a very specific meal plan, where I only ate things that this company sent me in the mail, so we couldn't go to the cabin until I did address-forwarding at the post office. And would there be address-forwarding if the beasties in the Capitol took over the government? Would the postmaster general of the Confederacy make sure I got my protein bars on time? I'm leaning toward no.

No shade to anyone who has a Plan, but Prepping as a formal hobby makes no damn sense to me. You're hoarding gold and ammo just waiting for the Apocalypse Walmart to open up? Loading in stacks of canned goods you intend to eat for the rest of your life? When the ish hits the fan, you're giving your Grandmeema a rifle to ward off marauders who are trying to steal the family chickens? This is what you're preparing for?

It's simply unacceptable. I won't accept it.

As I understand it, Prepping is intended to help you survive the end of society or, perhaps, the world. But what I'm saying is, if you're willing to consider such things—which I am not—you ought to have higher standards. Demand better of your end of the world. You really want to be eating canned peas while Grandmeema tussles with Mad Maxes out on the front lawn? Yikes.

What you need when society collapses is a new society—collective action and community responsibility and all that. Not walking down a dirt road toting a raccoon skin, six bullets, and a looted bottle of P. Diddy–brand vodka you're hoping to trade for some insulin.

Of course, the apocalypse will be seated according to class. Some people will be in their billionaire bunkers in Montana and Wyoming; we already know this. And some will board a yacht and sail across the melted ice caps until they run out of crudité and things get bleak. But for the rest of us, I guess it's useful to have a Plan. Which is embarrassing to me!

In my first book, I wrote about the end of the world and various doomsday scenarios. I did it as a way of engaging with my desire to hope and the sure knowledge that all of this is going to end. It was my way of holding my hand over a candle flame, thinking if I could make doomsday funny, the constant fear of death, tragedy, and loss wouldn't have power. This is joking as an anti-purgatory, a release from experiencing mortality as one long middle.

I name-checked a few scenarios (pandemic, ice age) that seemed too cinematic to occur and skipped over a few that seemed a little too likely for comfort (white people go buck-wild). I declared—cavalierly, in retrospect—that I did not have any desire to survive. I do not want to be in the post-apocalypse. I said remember me fondly when they're still doing TV tributes. I said I didn't want to be Patient Zero but I'd be Patient Fifty. I don't want to see the end of the world. I don't even want to see the flash of the nuclear bomb. I want to be making tea one minute and the next minute wake up in glory, as the old church folks used to say.

It just seems like a lot of stress. Like, beyond the obvious problems with post-apocalyptic survival (smelling bad, no TV, the fact that bartering with a bunch of traumatized pirates seems *so* annoying), I think the biggest thing in the cons category is the stress. I'm stressed enough as it is and most of my life is spent in air-conditioned environments. I have panic attacks for no reason. I haven't had a good night's sleep since Sasha Obama lived in the White House. (Please don't tell me to take melatonin to sleep; it makes me feel insane. And please don't tell me to smoke weed; I have never been more stressed than I was when high. I imagined a giant panda bear sitting in my closet, socking its fist into its open palm and glowering at me. Weed presented me with both the stress of a predator and the stress of the idea that a stranger was mad at me!)

I am stressed enough in the good times! I come from a long line of extremely anxious people. And my anxiety really has a lot of nerve, considering that my generation has it better than anyone else in our bloodline for at least the last four hundred years. Am I my ancestors' wildest dream? Babe, I don't know. I'll settle for being my ancestors' weirdest dream. I'm the dream my ancestors had when they got indigestion.

Being alive, I decided, when writing my little end-of-the-world essay for my first book in 2019, was stressful enough. I decline more stress! When the sea levels rise or the pandemic hits or the one-sided race war begins, I'm opting out of it for self-care reasons.

I still stand by this, even though it sounds coarser than I'd intended it when we all felt a bit more invincible, despite all of the threats to our health and well-being that existed in the times we were living. I meant it when my book came out in February 2020. And then, as tends to happen, February 2020 turned to March 2020. And I don't need to remind you what happened in March 2020.

People would send me DMs with screenshots of the pandemic portion of my book like "uh . . . thoughts?" I'd written an essay that might as well have been called "My, What Lovely Icebergs!: My Reflections on the First VHS of the Movie *Titanic* Prior to Watching the Second VHS." And meanwhile, locked down in my apartment, I'd be putting on a festive blazer, slathering my skin with some Fenty Beauty foundation that probably expired a year earlier, turning on the Zoom for one of the bright spots in my days: book clubs for my book that just happened to have an essay saying I did not want to be around during times exactly like this. And then I'd turn off the lights and bleach every surface in our apartment and listen to our neighbor coughing through the walls and spy on the people illegally using the building courtyard to walk their dogs and consider sewing my own mask but ultimately decide that learning a helpful domestic skill like a homesteader is too close to actually being post-apocalypse material. And I am not post-apocalypse material. I don't want the stress of it. I don't want to prepare. So what was I doing here?

I'd stare at my face in the mirror as I washed off my expired foundation, my existential terror never getting in the way of my desire to be thought of as someone whose pigmentation is consistent. My constant grief never stopped me from appreciating a conversation about my book, which always turned into conversations about hope, about how worthwhile it was to stick around, about seeing yourself in the future. I'd look into my own eyes in the bathroom that I occasionally did radio interviews in—for the acoustics, but mostly just to have a change of scenery—and I'd mutter, "You said you didn't want to survive, and yet here you are, you stressed-out traitor."

I did want to survive. I talked of hope because I wanted to survive. I opened a new document on my laptop because I wanted to survive. I bought an axe because I wanted to survive. I texted my brother back and waited for the car because I wanted to survive. I would go to the mountains to survive or stand in the middle of the street to survive. I would, I realized, do anything in my power to stay here. I found my capacity for tiny apocalypses to be shockingly large. I kept thinking, *Things are bad, but they're not the worst. This is not the end. The best . . . is yet . . . to come?* I wanted to survive. How embarrassing.

Soft Ground: An Interlude

"She often spoke to falling seeds and said, 'Ah hope you fall on soft ground,' because she had heard seeds saying that to each other as they passed."

— Zora Neale Hurston, *Their Eyes Were Watching God*

When the ground thawed late in the winter of 2021, David started digging a pond. He'd mapped it out when we first moved in. A cold bite still lingering in the air, he set about making the dream real. He didn't even say anything beforehand. He just walked out with a shovel one day and started to dig a hole meant to hold a thousand gallons of water. It was impressive to me but also quixotic. He'd later tell me that it was the only thing that would clear his head of the worry and stress that were overwhelming him from work and the world. He was trying to dig himself free.

We were still doing Zoom church together every Sunday from the house, and during the week, he was managing a food bank and grocery-delivery service out of the church and navigating the new world of pastoring remotely. The congregation had experienced a rash of deaths, none of them COVID-related, and it seemed like he was doing a Zoom funeral or a distanced burial at least once a month. He hadn't seen his parents face-to-face in over a year, both of them living in Oregon. Though he'd call and FaceTime, it wasn't clear when it would be safe to visit again. Even locally, with my parents, I'd mostly made do with driving down to Baltimore and standing by the car as I waved to them on their stoop, silent tears soaking my mask.

David turned thirty-five and I turned forty. I think we ordered takeout for one birthday. I might have bought crab cakes from Wegmans for my fortieth. Perhaps it's because of all that would happen soon after, but I don't remember a single thing about it.

Spring had not arrived bringing renewal.

So David dug. Silently, methodically, filling wheelbarrows with dirt. I wanted to help, but when I'd bend down, hot, jagged bolts of pain would carve a path across my lower back. When I lifted a garden tool, my elbow would throb and my arm would give out. I got to the point where I couldn't lift a hammer. I wanted to be out there with David. But I couldn't dig the pond for him.

Soon, the shape of the pond started to appear, and I got a sense of just how much work this was going to entail. It was supposed to be an immense pond, carved into a part of the sloping lawn that required digging down three or four feet in places to keep it level. He was going to be digging for months. Sometimes the way that I help in our relationship is by talking through logistics. Sometimes the way I help is by asking, "Could spending money change this situation?" So, after a few days of watching him dig for hours, I came out on the porch and called, "Do you want to get a backhoe?"

That's my marriage advice: When times get hard, rent some heavy machinery. It's probably best that David is the one who runs marital counseling.

Memorial Day came around and I was grumpy. We'd managed to procure the first vaccine dose and had tentative plans for our summer, but summer still felt far away. Everything in the present was just yard work and work work. And even the work work felt off. For years, I'd been developing my first book, *Here for It,* into a half-hour television comedy, and the producers I was working with had set me up with a network to pitch the series, in which a younger version of me would work at a community center next door to his parents' house. I was rehearsing constantly on my own and I had a big Zoom rehearsal with the producing team the next week. I was excited about it, but I was also very stressed. I'd started to feel like all of my work product was fake. It was like I'd forgotten how people functioned in real life and it was showing up in my scripts. I also felt so far removed from who I was and who I'd portray myself to be in the series—this lost kid who was going to find hope and community and, eventually, David. It's weird to create community when you're not in community. It felt fake to craft a happy ending while living outside the story you envisioned for yourself. I would write and rewrite and try to find the path.

With no meetings to attend, my thoughts that Memorial Day turned to the garden: an obligation and an obstacle. I bought fifteen bags of mulch from Lowe's that morning, because there was a sale and I am powerless against saving a small amount of money. I struggled to get them into the car and then struggled to unload them. I didn't understand why it was that David could look out at the yard and see a pond becoming and all I could see were weeds.

David was putting up netting around the marionberry bushes in the back. Cicadas were on the way, waking from a seventeen-year slumber and burrowing their way out of the darkness. The net was a two-person job, but he didn't ask for help and I didn't offer. I was shitty about the whole thing. We were silent all morning.

He came over to me after a few hours. "Can I talk to you?" he asked. I pulled out my earbuds. "I haven't been able to reach my dad for a couple of days, and I'm starting to get worried."

David was in the living room, sitting on the steps, calling Portland-area hospitals. I was in the kitchen, on the phone with David's mom, Rachel, who had driven over to David's dad's apartment to check on him. Though they were divorced, she had a key to his place and was David's first thought to ask for help. She interrupted herself mid-sentence.

"Oh, Eric. Call the police."

There is a before and there is an after. I hung up the phone. I started to shake, and my eyes welled up. I tried to pull myself together. I needed to cross the threshold into the living room, sit down, and tell my husband that his father was dead. What words are you supposed to use to do something like that? How do you begin the unimaginable?

"David," I started. "Hang up the phone."

I went upstairs to call my parents. "It looks like Rick had a heart attack," I said. "We're going to Portland tonight. We're staying with Rachel. Can you check on the house? I don't know when we'll be back."

I booked us flights for that night and packed a bag; we shut down the house as best we could. We threw all of the fresh produce in the composting, except for two peaches. I put them in my carry-on because David hadn't eaten. We drove off to the airport as the sun was starting to go down. The netting for the marionberry bushes hung off the trellis and bunched in the driveway, unfinished.

The Invitation

A few days after our engagement in 2015, David and I drove out to meet up with Rick, because Rick wanted to take us out on a boat to celebrate. Rick was one of those men who had loved fishing his whole life and did it whenever he could. And the plan was for David and me to meet him in Astoria, Oregon, on the Columbia River where it meets the Pacific, so that we could all go fishing together. This seemed like an intriguing idea at the time. True, I'd never had any interest in holding a fishing pole before in my life and—no offense to Jesus, famously the fisher of men—I thought it seemed like a boring pursuit. But I wanted Rick to like me.

There was no reason I couldn't do this. I liked fish plenty! I'd worked for an upscale seafood restaurant, so I knew many of their names and shapes. A great start. I went on a whale-watching trip in eleventh grade. We didn't see any whales, but I did meet my first drag queen. I wasn't sure if that information would be helpful on the fishing boat, but I'd be happy to volunteer it at any time. I'd watched *A River Runs Through It* and *The Voyage of the Mimi*. I was all set.

I'd only met Rick twice at that point, and he intimidated and fascinated me in equal measure. He'd been successful in the field of direct marketing at a time when it was still largely done through paper catalogs, brochures, and telemarketing. He worked for himself; he had side projects with other business partners, men and the occasional woman who knew money and influence; he was always looking for an investment.

Rick presented to me as the kind of Businessman that existed only in movies, the kind of guy who had a brick of a cellphone way before anyone else did and racked up frequent-flier miles in the hundreds of thousands and took clients out to steak dinners at exorbitantly expensive restaurants and understood mysterious words like "angel investors" and "EBITDA." I was, at the time, working as a program manager at an LGBTQ community center with a computer room full of giant donated desktops that got dripped on when it rained. I was an aspiring playwright with a laptop I'd bought off Craigslist; Rick was thinking of getting into drones.

Rick flew first-class even if, as I'd later learn, business was not as good as it had been. The industry was moving beyond him, and some bad investments had emptied his accounts. This frustrated David, understandably, but even before I knew this, I found the vestiges of the boom years that hung on him fascinating. To hear him talk, he was just one good investment or million-dollar idea away from changing everything again. What I admired was that it's possible that could be true. It had been once. He believed it could be again. He believed in himself. Rick spoke a language of finance and risk and the American Dream. Rick and I did not exist in the same universe.

Rick and David didn't always seem to exist in the same universe, either. David was a pastor who served housing-insecure people; he was getting his second master's, this one in therapy. David said that when they were together, Rick would goad him about politics, and they'd argue and argue. Rick could be hard, I'd learned, dogmatic and stubborn. He was more conservative than David and had taken a while to come around to

David's sexuality. If the fishing trip was any indication, he had changed his heart, but it had taken a lot of work on both sides. While I was dazzled by his business acumen and how strange his world seemed to me, I would soon learn how spiky the edges of the father–son relationship were and how easy it was to fall back into old patterns that were frustrating for both of them.

To my recollection, my father and I have never argued, so I didn't know how to navigate this kind of relationship as a son-in-law or partner. Everyone else's father is inscrutable to me. And this isn't a knock against other people's fathers. I just don't think we're set up, as a society, to see a lot of men in their complexity. And a lot of men aren't willing or able to show their complexity. And so we're left with a pile of tropes from the Father's Day card aisle at the supermarket: a reference to football, an old chair, a vague sentiment about working and sacrifice. Oh, and a mounted fish. Cuz men be fishin'.

David and I drove for a couple of hours through the dense greenness of western Oregon. I tried to figure out what kind of boat we were talking about here. Was this a rowboat? Would I need to paddle? David said it was a big boat, driven by someone else. There'd be a group of people, all fishing. That sounded fantastic. No physical labor on my part, a little champagne cruise. What a lovely hobby.

At one point, we got a strange text from Rick: *I'm going to Subway to pick up sandwiches for tomorrow morning. What kind do you want?* Why would I be eating day-old Subway sandwiches on a Columbia River champagne cruise? Then a second odd text came through. *Got a variety. They're in the cooler.* Okay, what was happening here?

Rick had booked David and me a room at a five-star establishment called the Cannery Pier Hotel, which remains one of the most gorgeous places I've ever stayed. It's right on the Columbia, with a view of the river and the Astoria–Megler Bridge. There were fresh cookies at check-in and the promise of free breakfast in the morning. Our massive room had a deck, and the bathroom had a soaking tub on a raised platform, with a window cut in the wall so that you could see over the bed, past the deck, and out onto the river as you bathed. This was luxury, honey! This was the kind of life I was trying to live! I was in heaven. I never wanted to leave the room. With my muscles aching from our climb up the mountain earlier in the week, I was looking forward to a good, relaxing soak and some leisurely boat-riding.

Rick sent another text while I ran water for the bath. *Meet in the lobby at 4:30 tomorrow. Need to get fishing licenses.*

"In the morning?!" I yelled through the bathroom viewing window, clutching the collar of my plush bathrobe. "What about the free breakfast?"

I have gotten up early for many things in my life, always against my will. But I have never had a harder time dragging myself out of bed and out the door than I did at the Cannery Pier. The sun wasn't up! Breakfast wasn't cooking! I'd only been there twelve hours, and in that time I'd only taken two baths! Why couldn't we have some fatherly bonding time by sitting in the nicest hotel lobby I've ever been in, ordering appetizers, and letting me talk about *The Voyage of the Mimi*? Luxuriating is my hobby. Getting free food is my hobby. Sleeping in is my hobby. I didn't voice any of this, because I didn't want to seem ungrateful, and I truly was grateful. Mostly for the bathtub with its own window. I was grateful for all of it. But I'd started to get a little worried.

At 5 A.M., we arrived in the darkness at a ramshackle building with a lit-up sign that read, ominously, TACKLE TIME. The shack sat alone on an empty pier, the only illuminated spot in an industrial expanse that looked like a nightmare out of a Stephen King novel. It had an ice cooler out front, its windows were covered in printed-out fishing regulations, and it gave off abandoned-gas-station vibes. I began to doubt that my morning was going to be spent sipping champagne.

We went inside and I surveyed the various lures, hooks, nets, and other serial-killer supplies they sold, while Rick bought David and me temporary angling licenses. Per the licenses, we were allowed to catch up to eight salmon on our excursion. That seemed ambitious given my level of skill and interest, but it was an honor just to be nominated.

Then we waited. The boat was leaving at 6 A.M. The clock read 5:15; it was not yet tackle time. Rick handed us Subway sandwiches from a cooler.

You will be shocked to discover that the boat was not a two-level riverboat with a big Proud Mary wheel at one end. It was a—how do I put this?—fishing boat. Like the one on *The Perfect Storm*. It had a simple navigation bridge with a console and a bearded man smoking a cigarette at the wheel. The deck was large enough to fit us and the other eight fishers, plus the three college-aged guys who were there to assist. There were fishing poles attached at regular intervals along the sides. I was informed that, once we were out in open water, we'd put the lures on the poles, drop the lines in the water, and wait.

Everyone else on the boat was white. All but one were men. They all had the craggy features and hangdog expressions that one might call salt of the earth. I don't really know what that phrase means, to be honest. They looked like people who had spent a lot of time getting blasted by water and sun on fishing boats. They were salt of the sea.

Each of the other fishers had a cooler with beer and, I presumed, Subway sandwiches.

We set out at six o'clock on the dot. The sun had just appeared in the distance. The sky had lightened to a pale blue with patches of wispy gray clouds near the horizon. It was gorgeous, serene. I didn't miss the riverboat dream so much. Besides, the plan was that we'd go out past where the Columbia meets the Pacific, drop anchor in a good spot, fish, and then return. With all the poles attached to the side, it seemed the only thing that would be simpler was if we just dropped a big net and scooped a bunch of fish up. Breakfast ended at ten at the hotel, which was four hours away. I got excited, because we'd clearly be back with plenty of time to grab it.

It took us maybe twenty minutes to get out to the ocean; all the while, David and I happily took photos and spotted birds along the coastline. The moment we hit the ocean, however, a wall of fog rolled in around the boat, blocking the view. It got a little choppy but nothing I couldn't handle. I was from an urban area adjacent to the Chesapeake Bay, after all. I was basically a merman. We dropped anchor, we all put lures on our respective lines, and with the *plink* of the hook dropping into the water I felt a wave of intense seasickness wash over me, from my head to the bottoms of my feet. I was suddenly so dizzy I had to grip the rail and sit down. My stomach convulsed, nauseous and churning. I didn't have to vomit, which in retrospect made it feel worse. All the parts of the seasickness were happening inside, with no way out. I was gobsmacked by how quickly it had happened and how wretched I felt. It was like someone was holding me upside down by my ankle and shaking me. I curled up in a ball on a bench, my stomach cramping violently, and tried to stifle my moaning so as not to scare away the fish.

David guessed that since the fog was blocking my view of the horizon, my body had gotten off-kilter and decided to kill me. I tried to play it cool, as I didn't want these fisher-people and the college-aged helpers to think less of me. But the nausea was relentless. I blew short bursts of air through my lips like I was giving birth. It didn't seem to help. I tried to talk myself down. We just had to catch some fish and then we'd go back. I could tough it out for another hour or so.

Poor David always wants to be helpful and realized that there was nothing he could do. I told him to abandon me and go hang with his dad. I would try to suffer inconspicuously.

At some point during my ordeal, the line on my fishing pole started wriggling, and everyone on the boat yelled at me to go pull the fish up. I was like, "Okay, well, I'm really just here for the experience. I don't have a need for a fish, but thank you!" They were undeterred, so I peeled myself off the bench, lurched over to the rail, and resentfully wound the spool until a fish appeared. I went to reach for it but one of the college-age helpers swooped in, scooted me out of the way, and took over. My hard work of winding some fishing line around a spool completed, I collapsed back onto the bench. Soon, David had caught a fish, as had Rick and the rest of the fishers on the boat. I perked up a bit, anticipating that we'd be pulling up anchor any minute and returning to shore and visible shoreline. But . . . that didn't happen. We just kept sitting there. People put new lures on their lines, cracked open new beers, and waited. I stumbled over to David. "WHY AREN'T WE LEAVING?"

He told me that the license allows each member of the boat, including crew, to catch eight fish, and so the way it works is that we sit there and we catch *eight fish* for each person on the boat. We could not leave until there were eighty-eight salmon on the deck of the boat. Some would catch more and some might catch fewer, but we'd all be leaving there with eight salmon each. You get a fishing license and suddenly everyone's a socialist.

I started to panic about the prospect of our time on the boat. I turned to the blank wall of fog over the bow and considered jumping into the sea and swimming back. I noticed that my phone somehow still had service, and my first thought was, *I need to call my mom to come pick me up.* This wasn't even hyperbole. An entire day of intense seasickness and occasional spooling loomed ahead of me, and I doubted I could take it. I really was going to ring my mom, who was at the time touring Oregon wineries with my Aunt Pat, and tell her, "Mommy, you need to rent a riverboat and get here stat. Also, please see that they've stocked champagne." I would have tried anything just to get some relief.

Across the boat I saw an older man taking his sweet time pulling up a rigid line. It started to get slack; the fish was getting away. I leapt across and shoved him out of the way. "You need to put your back into it, buddy. We can't afford to let any of these suckers get away. We have seventy-five fish to go! Playtime is over! It's tackle time now!"

Every time my line would jiggle, I'd lumber over to it, summon all the waning energy I had left, and attempt to cajole a fish on board. When other people struggled with their lines, I maniacally jumped up and helped. One time I jerked the line too much, lost the fish, and the hook came sailing back toward me. I closed my eyes and grabbed the railing to steady myself. When I opened them, I looked down at my wrist and found the hook sticking out of my flesh. There were no fish in there! I ripped it out and threw it back in the water; maybe the blood would help us catch a piranha. This was not a time to be picky!

I became a championship fisherman out of desperation. The others must have thought there was no one on that boat who loved fishing more than me, a man veering wildly between staggering around like he'd just left a New Year's Eve party and slumping over on a bench. It's all part of the process, folks! You've got to trick the fish into thinking that you have died of dysentery. Hours ticked by. I didn't say a word. My whole life was misery fishing. Later, David told me that Rick said to him, "Eric's very shy, isn't he?" which is the first time that's ever been said.

David replied, "Dad, he's really seasick!"

Rick had no idea. And that, my dears, is why I'm known as the greatest actor of my generation!

Rick came over and said he felt bad for bringing me out. I looked up at him weakly and said, with as much sincerity as my atrophying body would allow, "I am having a wonderful time."

I meant it, too. As much as I felt like a skeleton trying to break out of a flesh prison, I was still so grateful to be there and so touched to be included in this strange, beautiful, masculine morning of spooling threads. Rick *loved* fishing, and he wanted to share that with me. What a gift. I tried to put as much of that meaning into my voice as I could. I knew sometimes these things need to be clear. "I'm having a wonderful time," I said again.

I was reminded then of a moment at the end of my first date with David. I'd walked with him from the restaurant, our conversation continuing at the same pace it had for the last four hours. He lived past Rittenhouse Square, on the west side of

Center City Philadelphia. I lived in South Philly. We got to Broad Street, the dividing line, where I should have turned to go home, and I just kept walking. I didn't want to stop talking. And I'd been on enough nice first dates to know that what can seem idyllic and aligned at dinner can peter out over ever-more-sporadic texts the next week. I wanted to find a way to say, "I am having a wonderful time; let's not be strangers ever again." We kept walking. We crossed Rittenhouse Square; I had absolutely no plan. I told myself I was walking him home like a chivalrous suitor in the 1900s. I'd doff my straw hat, give a nod to the marm chaperoning all the debutantes in the house, and be on my way.

"Wait," David said in the middle of the park, "where do you live?"

Caught! "I live in South Philly," I said. "In the other direction. I'm just being weird."

David stopped and looked me in the eye. "I had a really great time," he said.

"Me, too," I offered. It's what you always say at the end of dates.

David kept looking me in the eye. "I had a really great time," he said again, and there was something in his voice—a sincerity and a vulnerability and an ardency—that told me it wasn't just a pleasantry, that he really meant it, and that he wanted me to know he meant it.

"I did, too," I said, trying to match his tone.

"Let's do this again."

And then we split and went our separate ways.

I said before that one thing led to another with us, like dots on a map. And that's true. But without the intention—that moment of saying, "I am telling you the truth and I hope that you can hear me"—I don't think any of this would have happened.

God in the Machine

The paperwork is the thing that gets you. Death is made up of a thousand transactions. Or maybe it's life that's made up of transactions. Death is a thousand receipts. Before we'd taken off from Baltimore en route to Portland, David had started a document on his phone with important information that would help with the mountain of work that came with his dad's death—dates, phone numbers, access information, to-do's. He knew going in that there would be a Zoom funeral service because of COVID restrictions. He knew that Rick wanted to be aquamated, the shorthand name for alkaline hydrolysis, a process that breaks the body down like cremation but by using water instead. And he knew that Rick wanted his ashes to be given a Viking burial in the water near his family's summer house in Maine. He shared this with me on our layover, then he went back to his phone and finished an Etsy search for a boat that could hold an urn and be set ablaze when the time was right.

A few years earlier, Rick had been diagnosed with cancer, and he and David had had conversations about what Rick would want to happen upon his passing. Through his work as a pastor, David had had end-of-life conversations and carried out end-of-life wishes dozens of times. Over the previous year, he'd buried beloved members of the congregation and walked their families through this process, even as he navigated his own grief. He knew by heart the questions to ask and the logistics to think through. I find that a marvel. I've never asked what those questions are or how to have those conversations. I've refused, when considering my own mortality, to decide what my wishes are. Sometimes I think it's because I'm still clinging to a phase of life where I can dupe myself into believing I'll live forever. Other times I think it's because I'm ambivalent about what happens to my body once the soul is gone. Isn't it none of our business? There are songs that I'd like played at my funeral, but I hesitate to make them known for fear that they mean something only to me. What if I compose a playlist and it has the effect of trapping a friend in a car and forcing them to listen to the random tune I'm obsessed with? I've done this, actually, to David on road trips. "Isn't this amazing?!" I call over the sound of the stereo blasting. He indulges me. But I'll be very surprised if, when it's all over, he opts to queue up Fleetwood Mac's "Tusk" as my ashes are spread. I guess we'll find out. Rick and David hadn't chosen to wait and see. They'd talked it out. There's nothing that can prepare you, really, but there is paper.

The first full day in Portland, we went together to pick up another Etsy purchase, an urn made from a gnarled, twisted piece of driftwood. Rick and David shared a love of the outdoors, and David wanted an urn that reflected it and that wouldn't disrupt a natural element when returned to the water in Maine. The seller arranged to meet us in the parking lot of a Sonic Drive-In, which made it feel like a high school drug deal. I sat in the car like a gangster's moll while a guy with a salt-and-pepper ponytail pulled up in what he'd described to David as a "hyper blue" Honda. There was a tiny champagne-colored corgi in the back seat, looking thrilled with life. We strapped the urn into the back seat of Rachel's car.

The major business of the day was seeing to Rick's apartment. We'd need to collect personal effects, figure out what to do with the rest of his belongings, and turn the apartment back over to the leasing company. Because it was the first of June, we knew that Rick had already paid for the month. But we weren't going to be out there for a month. We weren't sure how long we were going to be in Oregon, but when we left, the apartment had to be done. David knew that he would need to find whatever papers and files he could that would help him close Rick's accounts and turn matters over to probate court. I knew, having moved three times in the preceding four years, that the work of packing up and cleaning can quickly become overwhelming. I couldn't help with so much of what he was doing, but I decided I could do this part. I could deal with the other stuff. The rest of the life.

We'd been warned that there was a lot to be sorted through at Rick's apartment, but my first impression of the complex was that it was idyllic, nestled into a sprawling forest in Lake Oswego overlooking the Willamette River. Rather than one towering apartment building, the complex was made up of small clusters of eight units, four stacked in a square facing another four across a small courtyard. They looked like treehouses, with external wooden staircases and branches brushing against the windows and sunlight streaming white and green through the leaves. We found Rick's unit tucked at the end of a winding drive shaded by vine maples and towering ponderosa pines. It was peaceful. It was perfect.

Once inside, I hung back while David got the lay of the land and figured out the next step. It was an unexceptional two-bedroom apartment—the charm was the location—and Rick hadn't been there but a few years, so the decor was simple. Entertainment center, overstuffed recliner, bed and dresser, rowing machine. I started to make mental notes, knowing that not now, not today, but soon, we'd have to figure out where it all would go. Most striking, however, was that every surface—the dining room table, the kitchen counter, the desk—was covered with loose stacks and plastic bins full of paper. Bank statements and receipts and tax forms and printed emails and old catalogs. An entire life. We went to the office and found the closet piled high with more bins, decades and decades of work product from an age and an industry that was all paper. He'd saved everything. And we would have to go through everything, stack by stack, bin by bin, to determine what needed to be kept and what should be shredded.

David went next door to meet the neighbor while I started to clean out the kitchen cabinets, filling up bags and walking them down a path covered in pine needles to a dumpster in the parking lot. When I came back, the neighbor, a young-faced man with white hair, and David were inside the apartment and the neighbor was saying that the four renters who lived on the upper floor of this little village had gotten to know each other during COVID by talking from their staircases, their voices echoing in the treetops. David was quiet, focused like a laser, as he would continue to be in the coming days. He was holding on to everything, too.

We went across the courtyard to see another neighbor, a woman who was in the midst of packing. She'd come from the Midwest after the dissolution of a thirty-year marriage and was now on her way to California. She had silhouette appliqués of dandelions on her walls and quotes about being magic. "I liked Rick," she said as she beckoned us in through the insect screen at her door. "A real character. Grumpy old guy!" She told us that she went over to feed Rick's cat, an indoor/outdoor Maine coon, or to clean up for Rick sometimes. "And I'd snoop," she said unapologetically. "The only thing on his wall was your wedding announcement from *The New York Times,* in a frame. He was really happy for you."

We couldn't figure out how to contact the leasing company, so we just walked through the complex until we found the office in a locked building with a sign on the door that gave instructions for dropping off rent checks and modified procedures for COVID safety. A young woman in yoga pants and a crop-top hoodie came out to meet us. She was shocked by the news. "I really liked Rick," she said. "Funny. It's hard—this is one of those places people move to and then die. I've lost a few, but Rick was one of my favorites." David listened. The intensity was starting to worry me. I would later ask whether he felt like people were processing at him, as I've seen people do before in other circumstances. He has a kind face and pastoral energy; people want to seek refuge in him. He told me that he didn't feel like he was on the job. He wanted to know it all. He wanted this kaleidoscopic view of his father and the dimension that other people's emotions added to his own. At a time when every part of his life was devoted to logistics and lists, their feelings were welcome.

We left the apartment for the day, exhausted and over-whelmed by the tasks ahead. We weren't sure of so many things that we needed to know about, from questions as mundane as how to cancel his cable to information as crucial as who else was in his life who might call or drop by or be expecting him in a day or so. We didn't know whether he had ongoing business dealings or accounts that needed to be turned over to probate. We didn't know if there were debts or commitments or anything. There wasn't a will. There was just forty years' worth of paper. David took Rick's phone and laptop and drove back in Rachel's car. I drove Rick's compact, sporty Mazda, which we found in the parking lot. There was a bag of nonperishable groceries in the back—cat food, paper towels, a bag of Milano cookies.

How much of your life is a mundane mystery to other people? We'll share the events of our days over dinner or call our parents to update them on the highlights, but there are all the little details and interactions that fill in the cracks in our lives. Who are the people in your phone address books and emails? What are the appointments in your calendar and the small notes that make sense only to you? What is the song that is wafting through your head? What about the people you see every day—cashiers and fellow commuters and neighbors— who might realize they miss you but never really know what happened? There was paper, so much paper, but aren't these little facts, unremarkable but crucial, also receipts?

We tried to piece together the ineffable while addressing what was still mysterious but slightly more knowable. For instance, as Rick knew from a professional life spent researching people's buying habits and reaching out to them by phone and by email, there'd be a web of companies and agreements and log-ins and mailing lists attached to his name. Some of them David would need to disentangle, others would just continue in perpetuity.

A few years earlier, I went back to Oregon with David to watch him get a young alumni award from his college. We met up with Rick the day before and had dinner. Money was tight and Rick was stressed about it. His thoughts kept coming back to this real estate deal he'd gotten into or potentially wanted to get into. It wasn't clear. In addition to direct marketing, he'd also had his real estate license for years, and at various points there'd been developments or projects or investments, some of which paid off, many of which did not. Rick was always about to turn it around. I tried to follow the conversation, but it was hard. I didn't understand the kind of business that he did. I didn't understand the stakes. Then he and David got into a back-and-forth about politics—Rick started it—and I got very tense. When the server came over to offer dessert, they declined and, against my nature, I declined, too, thinking we'd soon end the uncomfortable dinner. But they kept at it for another forty-five minutes, and I just sat there and looked out the window, so heated about not having a piece of cake.

The next day we drove out to the college, and Rick was waiting in the event space when we walked in. There was a cluster of people by the podium, and David joined them to check in and do a soundcheck for his speech. I hung back with Rick. He seemed to be in his own world, and I was uncomfortable. As much as I liked him, I still didn't really know what to say to someone else's dad, and the memory of the dinner was fresh. I threw out a simple "How's it going, Rick?" and he launched into a stressed monologue about the investment and his business partners and how one had screwed the rest of them over.

It was a lot, and even as he was saying it, I was thinking, *I have no idea how to respond to this.* I kept nodding and listening as I turned to watch the soundcheck. One of the honorees moved and I noticed a woman with shoulder-length blond hair facing the stage, with her back to me. I'm going to preface this by saying I've thought about this for years and I have no explanation for it, but I promise you it happened just like this. I saw the back of this woman's head and my brain said, *Oh! That's*

Cheryl Strayed! I'd read Cheryl's books; I followed her advice column *Dear Sugar;* I'd seen *Wild,* the Reese Witherspoon movie based on her memoir. But I don't think I was walking around with a working knowledge of what Cheryl Strayed looks like. I don't know what most authors look like. And I definitely don't know what the backs of their heads look like. But something about this woman's hair reminded me of one person in the world, and that's Cheryl Strayed.

Without taking my eyes off the woman, I became aware of Rick again. "So anyway," he was saying, "I think the mob is going to come after me." Now both my eyes and my ears had information they couldn't process. The woman turned her head toward me. It *was* Cheryl Strayed. I got giddy.

"Listen, Rick, hold that thought. I've got to go talk to someone."

I scooted across the room. I still don't know what was going on in that story. Suffice it to say, the mob did not come knocking.

Cheryl's husband was getting an award from the alumni association, too, and afterward Cheryl complimented David on his speech and introduced us to her two kids. She told a funny story about talking about the concept of religion with her kids, and that led us into a conversation about Noah's Ark. The kids asked what that was, and Cheryl said to David, "Well, you can tell it better than I," which, coming from Cheryl Strayed, is the highest compliment a storyteller can receive.

Then, off the cuff, David told the most wise and beautiful rendition of the Noah's Ark story I've ever heard, adding context both historical and literary, and ending with the rainbow. "It's a symbol of God's promise to us not to destroy the world again. It's a bow, like a bow and arrow, and it's turned toward God rather than earth to show the seriousness of the promise." My jaw fell open. I'd never heard that before.

One of Cheryl's kids asked, "So, is that true?"

And David smiled, ever the pastor, the budding youth minister or father or friend, and said, "Well, that's the question, isn't it? What do you think?" And then the four of them had a long, robust conversation about the use of stories and myth and the promises we make to each other in the midst of destruction and the promises that we assume life has made to us.

We were running late to the appointment with the funeral director, where David would sign some paperwork, pay for the aquamation, and do Rick's final viewing. We sat in traffic, and stress filled up the air in the car to the point where it was stifling. I gingerly tried to suggest to David that funeral directors are probably quite used to people running late or being all over the place, but I had no idea if that was true or not. And I knew that it was a cold comfort anyway, since the stress wasn't so much about being late as it was the magnitude of what was about to occur. I had no idea what we were walking into. I had no idea what it would feel like, and by that third day everything had started to seem surreal. I saw our actions as through mottled glass, with no frame of reference for anything. So I focused on the smallest tangible tasks, totems from the real world. David had figured out a date for the Viking funeral in Maine, so I'd made flight arrangements and booked a car rental. I looked up Goodwill donation centers and paper-shredding facilities, knowing that at some point the papers would be sorted through and I would take over and remove them. I'd paid our bills. I rehearsed my pitch for my TV series over and over again and answered emails, unsure of why I was still working but at a loss for a reason not to when David wasn't home. Nothing felt real. Nothing except this.

The funeral director was busy when we arrived, so we were led to the chapel by an apprentice, who the director would later tell us was the best embalmer he'd ever encountered. She seemed young, maybe late twenties, but she was wearing a mask, like we were, so I couldn't say for sure. She had slicked-back hair that was shaved on the sides and wore a stylish long black over-coat over black slacks and a white button-down. I immediately got Dr. Who vibes from her. I was dazzled. Her name, delight-fully and anachronistically, was Ethel.

"He's right through here, my darling," she said to David as we walked across the parking lot. Her voice was very soft, al-most in a saccharine way, but genuine. She spoke like a kinder-garten teacher, which I found fascinating. This was beyond the muted tones of funeral-director speak; there was a level of sweet and disorienting intimacy to the way that Ethel spoke that felt wholly new.

As we walked, she began to casually rattle off disclaimers in that same tiny, mellow voice. "I washed him up real good," she said proudly. "There might be some soap left on his chest be-cause it smells good. I had to put a little bronzer on him, but he looks great. I brushed his teeth up nice and clean, but his tongue might stick out." It was a very kind monologue of non sequi-turs. But the information, as I was receiving it, sounded hor-rific. The body in parts. The process as a matter-of-fact task list. What does it mean? What am I supposed to do with this? Was what she was saying true? She continued to describe Rick's appearance with the gentle lilt of a fairy-tale narrator.

Inside the chapel building, David asked her to prep me for what I was going to see, which is a gesture of such thoughtful-ness that it still takes my breath away. I had decided that I wouldn't ask any questions and I'd deal with whatever we were walking into because it wasn't about me. But David knew that

I didn't regularly encounter death and dead bodies. He knew, in a way that no one else does, that I avoid it. I won't acknowledge its reality. I don't approach caskets; I sit far back at funerals if I go at all. I am purposefully unprepared. He knew that and he wanted to help me, at this time when I was supposed to be helping him. I think that might be what marriage is.

In response to David's request, Ethel again launched into a litany of facts that was so strange to me that I started to panic. I couldn't form a mental picture. I didn't know what was going to be behind the door.

But, of course, when she unlocked the door to a small, warmly lit viewing room, I saw: It was Rick. No, it was Rick's body, wrapped in a shroud and covered by a quilt. But he looked wonderful, a small smile across his lips.

I immediately started to cry. And I was so furious with myself for it. Why couldn't I just hold it together? Why couldn't I just be there for David? David kept checking on me, which was so kind. I wanted better for him.

We put some flowers around Rick, framing his face. After a few moments, I stepped outside to give David time alone. I sat in a pink mausoleum on a pink marble bench. There were flowers all over the floor in vases, many of them fake. I think they must have been left over from Memorial Day. Most of the markers on the walls around me were for people who died in the sixties or seventies. There were a couple of plaques where one member of a couple died in the sixties and the other member died in the 2000s. That's how it goes sometimes, but it was still curious to see.

Ethel came over and handed me a note for David that told him she was going to go do some work, but he should call her when he was done so they could "powwow" about doctors. They needed to find one of Rick's doctors who could sign off on the death certificate. I realized that this was information that I actually had, so I ran after her, desperate to be helpful in some way. David came out then and asked for directions to a trash can.

"In the bathroom, pumpkin," she replied, pointing to a corner. Pumpkin. I looked at her in her Dr. Who coat with bemusement, like she was someone who had just stepped out of a spaceship. I could not believe that any of this was real.

That first week stretched into two. We held a funeral over Zoom from Rachel's living room. I made daily trips out to the apartment, where David and Rachel would sort through papers, and I'd take them to be shredded. My arms, legs, and back, already so wrecked from the yard work, burned constantly with pain from lifting and bending. There was so much to be done, and it seemed to be getting more complicated, not less. I spent two days trying to get the cable cut off. They told me I needed to put it in my name and send a death certificate before they could do it. I thought, *That can't be right*. I found another way that is probably not wise to put in print. The indoor/outdoor cat came home. The neighbor took him in. My mother checked in by phone every day. I usually talked to her at Rick's, where I was often alone. I told her about the stress that David was under, the different kind of stress that I was under. How everything felt overwhelming. She talked to me every day about the mysterious and confusing process of helping a partner navigate grief over a parent's death. All you can do is just be present with them, she said, whenever and however it shows up.

David navigated all of the business, big and small, that Rick had left behind. I tried, ever so gently, to keep us on a schedule with closing down the apartment. I didn't want to rush him, but at some point we'd have to go back to the other parts of our lives. As if there was a clear delineation or a way to return. My whole life, my other life, was only reachable through the screen. Just as it had been for the previous sixteen months of quarantine. But this felt different. Everything was remote. The beauty of modern times is that it doesn't matter where you are. You can be anywhere. But the beauty of life is that sometimes, the most important times, you have to actually be here.

In Baltimore, my mother went out to check on our house. She called me from the porch. The cicadas were everywhere. The grass was so tall it bent over.

The second time I met Rick, he took us out to lunch after David had given a talk at a TEDx event. David was still interning at a church, and I was working in management at a theater. We didn't have any money whatsoever. For months, I'd been in the process of applying for a job I really wanted. It paid more, it seemed to be the right move for me, and it aligned with the person I was trying to be then. I'd applied, submitted secondary materials, interviewed. I made the final two and then . . . nothing. They were still deciding, they said. For weeks. Then months. It had gotten to the point where I was getting deeply discouraged, because the lack of decision had started to feel personal. Why wasn't I good enough to say yes to? What about me inspired such indifference? Why couldn't I seem to move ahead in my career?

David went to the bathroom during lunch and, like a witness in an interrogation room, I started just spilling my guts to Rick out of nerves.

He looked at me appraisingly and then said, "You need to write them a letter and give them an ultimatum."

I nodded obediently, but then I said, "Yeah, I don't know if that's a great idea for me."

He apparently wasn't looking for feedback at this time, because he continued, "You need to tell them that they're not going to find anyone better than you, they're crazy to be jerking you around like this, and that if they don't hire you, they're going to regret it. Then tell them that they need to respond to you by next week."

In the moment, I thought this was crazy. Rick was a tall, white baby-boomer businessman who'd made his money sending paper to people and calling them on the phone and getting them to buy things. This seemed to have no application to the world of nonprofit management. I was begging for a job that would pay me forty thousand dollars a year. We did not live in the same worlds.

After we'd parted ways, however, I thought about his advice, and I realized I had nothing to lose by being more assertive. I wrote what I felt at the time was the craziest, most audacious letter ever composed. I wrote a letter that was like, "Don't make me come down there and give you a piece of my mind. May I please have insurance and vacation days, dammit?!" I sent it. The nonprofit replied the next day. They offered me the job three days later. I couldn't believe that Rick was right.

Later, David told me that Rick liked that I was a worker bee. "He liked connecting with you about business," he said. I couldn't imagine that was true. I couldn't imagine how he saw me.

In that restaurant, he'd given his son's frantic boyfriend that age-old fatherly, business-y talking to, but he'd also given me the secret to his success: Send a letter, get a response. Remind them who the hell you are, even if you don't know yet. Reach out, show up.

————

We met the funeral director at the crematorium and waited with him, standing in a nondescript outer office that gave no indication of the building's purpose. Inside, the space looked like an accounting firm from the eighties, with fluorescent lights on low ceilings and two metal reception desks. One desk sat cluttered but empty; behind another, a receptionist was paging through a binder slowly. There were random plaques, advertisements, and signs on the wall. I was shocked by the generic, unremarkable energy of this place. This is where it ends?

Finally, a man in a cardigan and the most beat-up oxfords I've ever seen came out of a side office and led us down a short hallway, to a big metal door.

"It's a little industrial back here," he warned us, as he punched in a code and swung the door open. I quickly realized this was the same kind of soft-voiced underselling that Ethel had been well versed in. The back area was twice as tall as the front, concrete and cavernous. There were multiple hearses parked on the side and a few motorcycles. Once again, I became completely disoriented. It looked like a taxi garage. I was so overwhelmed by the size of it and the cars and the concrete nothingness. There was a mural on the wall next to the door we'd walked through. I turned and looked closer. It was actually a bunch of completed puzzles, glued together and mounted. What was the purpose? What were we doing here?

We turned to the left, and then we saw. Rick's body was lying in a shroud on an adjustable table, like a hospital gurney, about twenty feet away. There was nothing around him save for a sink against a wall, maybe ten feet beyond the gurney. And in the far-right corner, I intimated, there was an incinerator, though I refused to look closely. At first I didn't see the technician, so I got confused about how Rick had gotten there. Had we not done something we needed to do? Why were we seeing this? What was going to happen?

A curly-haired technician emerged from the sink area, wearing a medical gown and gloves. I realized the whole place had a strange smell, like an aquarium. My brain just said, *Sharks*. Maybe like a high school science classroom. Like formaldehyde, though green burial uses no formaldehyde. So, I don't know.

The technician asked David if he was familiar with the process. He said, "Yes, but go over it again." She said they'd put a metal grate on top of Rick—here she indicated the oxford-wearing hipster, who held up a slightly rusted grate, curved and human-length. I realized that Rick's table was composed of the bottom half. I was starting to get freaked out. She said they'd raise the table and put Rick in the machine. I noticed for the first time a machine to our left. It was a huge silver cylinder with wires and tubes coming out of it. It must have been fifteen feet long and stood just as high. It was mounted on a tripod of metal beams like a giant telescope. Between this contraption, the technician, the grate-holding assistant, the cavernous room, and the fact that we were all wearing masks, it had huge nineties kids-sci-fi-movie vibes. A *Honey, I Shrunk* situation. The technician said that after Rick was put in the machine, they'd tilt it at a forty-five-degree angle. And for some reason, this was the detail that broke me. The surrealness all became too much. The matter-of-fact statements. The clinical descriptions. No one was doing anything wrong, but I couldn't process the truth. I was not prepared for the science of death.

Later, I would go back and try to recall everything I'd seen and search the internet for information until it made sense. I needed to name things and to understand their purpose. I needed confirmation that what I'd seen was real. And I wanted, if only in retrospect, to be prepared. The grate, for instance, is called a harrow. When used as a verb, "harrow" means to cover, often with soil in a garden. It is a word that holds finality and potential equally.

How strange that a machine as futuristic-looking as the silver cylinder needed something as simple as a rusted harrow in order to run. How strange that, as the technician told us, the process of aquamation is the same as the process of decomposition, just accelerated—years shrunk down into hours. How strange that the body comes to this.

I tried to calm down. I held David's hand. He approached the body and said his goodbyes. Then he nodded at the technician, she started ratcheting up the table on hydraulics, and she and the assistant steered the unwieldy table toward the contraption.

David and Rick had chosen aquamation from this facility because, after the process is done, the ashes are returned to the survivors and the water is transported to a nearby forest. Part of Rick's physical form would remain with us, and the rest would be immediately absorbed into the soil, then the roots, the branches, the leaves.

They closed the hatch and spun the lock and then the machine started to tilt. The technician came over to David and told him that he could start the process if he wanted. He went over. I went with him, out of support and also curiosity. Was there a lever? A switch? There was a screen with a bunch of yellow and blue square buttons with rudimentary computer-font writing. The yellow button in the upper right-hand corner read "START." I didn't know what I expected it to say. But not that.

David pressed it. The machine whooshed to life. We stepped back. I presume water was rushing in around Rick. I tried to

picture it, but I couldn't. I didn't want to. It terrified me. I ignored the flood and thought of the rainbow and the promise it
made. I thought of the trees. I thought of Ethel performing care
for Rick's body and care for us. I thought of the stacks of paper.
I thought of the handcrafted wood urn. I thought of the grass
bending over in Baltimore. I thought of my parents at the door
to our house. I thought of the glow of television over Rachel,
David, and me after a long day. I thought of David's hand carefully picking out flowers to place around his father's face. I
thought about the tasks. All this work of love.

We watched the tilted cylinder for a while. Then David nodded and we left.

Rainbow Connection

The pond was a breathtaking wonder. David had finished work on it before we went to Oregon. He'd built a shallow beach area on one side for animals to enter and exit and carved a waterfall into the hill on the other side. It had an aerator that ran on solar power, and he'd ensured the pond's long-term viability by reinforcing it with waterproof tarp, wooden slats, and rebar. He filled it with plants, rocks, and, finally, water. We quickly realized that it would completely evaporate on hot days—a thousand gallons, Raptured! So he connected a hose to the waterfall and put it on a solar-powered timer to pull water from the well that also supplied our house. I thought it ironic that we'd done such a good job solving the flooding issues in the backyard that now we needed to add more water.

The front yard proved to be a different story. It still flooded, but we couldn't plant as much up there because we had to work around the underground septic tanks. Most of the overflow was caused by runoff from our neighbor's front yard. Their septic-system installation had raised their yard a foot and a half higher than ours, which caused a deluge whenever it rained. They were incredibly nice and hospitable people, perfect neighbors in every way. Without us even asking, they'd been extraordinarily helpful while we were away. But topographically they were menaces.

David did some research and decided to dig a trench between our yards so that the water could collect there. Another ditch! Eventually, he said, he wanted to put in a French drain from the backyard to the front, which is a pipe buried in the trench that funnels water from higher ground to lower ground. When he told me about this, I envisioned a plumbing innovation used by the characters in *Les Mis*. But apparently they're called French drains because they were invented by former U.S. assistant secretary of the Treasury Henry French. There's no musical about him, so I immediately stopped paying attention.

The trench ran the twenty feet from the back edge of the house to the road and went down about a foot and a half. After the first rainstorm, it immediately filled all the way up. So now we had a moat. The neighbor two doors up, who lived in the house where the gay couple had been, was a retired woman who liked to walk her dog through all the lawns on the street, which felt presumptuous to me but whatever. People just be doing all kinds of things in suburbs. Did I write about it on Nextdoor under a pseudonym? You can't prove it. When we put the moat in, I was concerned that she'd see it as an act of aggression or, worse, tumble into it. I planned to put down a little footbridge, or at least a plank of wood or something. Add a troll, collect a toll. That's the American way, baby! But before I had a chance to do anything, one morning I came downstairs in my underwear and encountered her right outside our front window; her dog was sniffing at the mailbox, clearly plotting to steal my identity. She waved to me brightly. What does one do here? I waved back. "Excuse my nipples and mind the moat!" I called.

David found a toad in the moat. It would occasionally croak in the evening, a gentle, low call. He bought it a toad house, which was basically an upside-down pot with a little door carved in it. He put the house by the moat and then, to lure the toad to the pond, he moved it slowly up the length of the garden. The toad seemed really pleased by this arrangement. I forwarded the toad our Airbnb code of conduct and informed him that there was a continental breakfast from "10-ish to whenever" every day if I remembered to serve it. Soon, the toad was joined in the pond by a tree frog that chirped brightly through the night. I was surprised by how far the frog's call carried. You could hear it in the house with the windows closed, which also felt presumptuous to me.

One night we were sitting by the pond, listening to the frog and the toad have a conversation out of an Arnold Lobel book. We became aware of the sound of another tree frog, coming from the home of the neighbor with the dog. Her house had a pool, and our next-door neighbors informed us that she hadn't maintained the pool upkeep. Before we'd arrived, the pool had turned green and filled with creatures.

The sound of the frog from the pool house was coming closer and closer, completing a call-and-response with our frog. Soon, David and I had to raise our voices a little to be able to hear each other. I commented on how lovely it was that these two frogs were falling in love right in front of us. David informed me that it's the male tree frogs who do the calling. We tried to find any female frogs in the pond, but it was just the lone male frog and the toad, with the other dude frog hopping his way across our neighbor's back lawn. Soon, they were in the pond together, loudly chirping in sync. "David," I said, "you've created an Amphibian Gay Bar." I'd never been prouder.

When we first met, I was working at an LGBTQ center, and he was an intern pastor leading an LGBTQ group at his church. We bonded over our shared love of creating spaces of belonging. But it seems we were a little too good at making queer community, because over the month of May, that Amphibian Gay Bar filled up with dozens of loud-ass homosexual frogs. They'd set up camp around happy hour, screaming at each other about how much they love Miss Piggy all night long. The East Coast tree frog has a high-pitched trill that can last upwards of thirty seconds; these weren't discreet chirps, they were monologues. It was so loud at times that David had to move his regular back-porch phone calls with his mom inside the house so he could hear her.

Then, other nights, there'd be no frogs at all. "I guess *Drag Race* is on," I said.

When we went to Oregon, I got a text from our next-door neighbors: *Your frogs are VERY loud.* I apologized profusely, but our neighbors assured me they were just kidding. They loved the sound.

Frankly, I thought this was madness. When we got back in June, David would be lulled to sleep by the incessant din of the screaming frogs. He said it relaxed him. Meanwhile, I heard it as shrieking. It didn't sound like they were a quarter acre away; it was as if all of the air around our house was frog chirps at full volume. The racket invaded every space in our home, overpowering the ambient burr of the air-conditioning, rattling through my skull at a frequency that not only kept me awake all night but intensely agitated me. It was high-pitched and constant, with all of the frogs chirping at different times to create a wall of sound that was crushing me. These were mating calls, but also, they were acts of terrorism. These horny gay frogs were trying to drive me insane.

I grew frenzied from lack of sleep and the psychological torture of queer amphibians clacking their fans and caterwauling all night. I took to googling "When will the frogs stop screaming?" at 4 A.M. every night. My search led me to message boards about decks and pools that had been invaded by frogs. There I found a bunch of folksy, bewildered Americans (and a large number of Australians, interestingly) who are bedeviled by this plague. And, from the jittery tones of their posts, the desperate measures they'd attempted, and the way that some of their sagas ended in numb admissions of defeat, it was clear that the frogs could not be stopped. You couldn't drive them out, and if they breached the house, you were done for. Abandon your land; it belongs to them. I felt fortunate that they were content to stay in the pond. I'd only found one frog on the porch, and I think I scared him off by bursting into tears.

During that summer, I was also working on a new play, called *Merland,* which imagines a pair of sibling mermaids who live at the bottom of a Baltimore reservoir. The play begins with their house being invaded by frogs, and one of those frogs becomes the chief antagonist of the play. Eventually, in that early draft, the frogs burn the house down. I'd written all of this before the pond was even begun, but as I sat awake, rocking on the floor, I began to wonder if I'd summoned it.

I read up on the life cycle of tree frogs as dawn tipped over the horizon. I learned that frogs return to the pond where they are spawned, which seemed like a useful metaphor to weave into the play and also a curse that was being put on our house. There were thousands of eggs in the pond now. Apparently, the frogs had turned to surrogacy and there would be no end.

After a week of me railing and lurching through the house like a madman, David bought me earplugs. The sound from the pond was so intense that I had to put in the earplugs and also put my head under the pillow in order to rest. "I support the rights of these gay frogs to congregate and raise their adopted tadpoles," I said to him as I stuffed multiple plugs into my ears.

"But I just don't know why they have to shove their lifestyle in my face."

I read on the forum that snakes chase off frogs, so I thought about buying some snakes. But that seemed likely to create another problem. Namely, that then I would have snakes. Another commenter said that if you sprayed vinegar on the ground around the pond, they wouldn't come in from the trees, because the vinegar would burn their skin. This felt like an extreme step. Was I really going to try to evict these frogs from the pond we built specifically for them? I'd lived in the suburbs for less than a year and already I'd pivoted to being very aggressive about borders. Vinegar was not just a remediation strategy; it was a litmus test of my morality. You cannot be a progressive and still cast out frogs!

I changed my political party and filled up a spray bottle.

It couldn't hurt to test a little area, I figured. Maybe it would deter the frogs without injuring them. I didn't want to close down the Amphibian Gay Bar, I just wanted to raise the property value so much that the Amphibian Gay Bar had to move. I wanted to turn the Amphibian Gay Bar into a trendy fusion restaurant and a high-rise luxury-condo building. Was that so wrong?

I sprayed a little vinegar near the beach and left a contrite note. "I support you. No H8!"

The next day David came to me, concerned. Some of the decorative grass by the pond had what looked like bleached spots on it and appeared to be dying. I had to sheepishly and apologetically admit to him that we weren't being beset by a mysterious plant disease. "It's my fault," I said. "I may have done a small act of frog homophobia."

———

A garden is supposed to relax you and feed you, I thought. Instead, it was again turning me into someone I didn't want to be. But now I wasn't just being punished by muscle aches and malaise, I was being beset by the plagues. At night, over the din of the frogs *kiki*-ing in the pond, I was kept up by my own voice asking one question in my head: *Have I failed?*

It wasn't just the killing of a small tuft of decorative grass. Nor was it my resistance to the frogs or my struggle to keep up with the mowing and the weeding and the harvesting. It wasn't that each part of the outdoor project seemed to bring David joy but trigger stress in me. It was the feeling that I was an unintentionally destructive force in this generative space. And if that was happening in the yard, then what was keeping it from our house and our shared dream? Was I failing us by letting my unhappiness in the garden cloud what we'd hope to create? Happiness. The holy grail of the last five years. The albatross. Must one *always* be *happy*?

Who am I? I asked myself. *Who am I now? Who am I now?* It was an echo of the frustrated refrain that crowded out the mindfulness practice my therapist Brian had suggested. In the noise, I searched for quiet in my thoughts.

I remembered the night that we came back from settling Rick's affairs in Oregon a few weeks earlier. We arrived at the house late at night. When the yard came into view, we both gasped in unison. Where previously there had been mulch and weeds, now the headlights of the car illuminated plants waist high in places—borage and dahlias and torch lilies and zinnias near the porch; asparagus and tomato vines and lacinato kale overflowing from the raised beds in the distance. The cicadas hadn't killed the marionberry bushes, and the plants' spiky, spindly arms hung from the trellis, over the crumpled net, and flopped onto the slate path. The grass was so tall the yard looked like marshland. At the pond, water lilies and cattails that David had just planted bloomed and shot up to the sky, waving in the night breeze. We pulled out our phones, turned on the flashlights, and ventured out.

The garden was incomplete and messy, but it was also beautiful. A creation that had demanded constant tending was flourishing now after being left alone. Some of the seeds we'd planted would outlast us. Beneath them, deep in the dirt, thousands of new cicadas were beginning a seventeen-year journey back to the surface. What world will we make by the time they arrive?

As if breaking a spell, one day the frogs were just gone. The forum to which I was a regular visitor by this point said it was normal; it was the end of mating season. The solution was just to leave them alone. They retreated from the yard all at once. Off to their rentals in Provincetown and Fire Island, I guess.

That night, David and I made dinner outside and sat at the pond. I've never been so grateful for silence. The sun went down and we stayed there. The fireflies came out, having hatched in piles of leaves David had collected the previous fall. He began telling me the names of the different types based on the way they glowed. I saw, through the flashes, the yard that we'd first planned for. Lush, and green, and bountiful, and easy. I saw the vision of the gazebo we'd talked about, lights strung along the eaves, a long banquet table in the middle. Everyone we love gathered around. The settings crowded with glasses and plates and elbows. The air filled with laughter, with stories, with each other's presence. Around the pond, and on the path, and all throughout the yard, we'd envisioned community. That's what we hungered for. I wanted to believe that that dream was still possible, even though the reality of making something new seemed more daunting now than it was before.

Oh God, to return. To find a way back to yourself, the version of yourself that wanted nothing more than what you have, the version of yourself paralyzed by the fear of living through what you've lived through, the stranger in your story who had just enough hope to make a path for you. But if we could go back, we'd never move forward.

I shook the dream out of my head and focused on the world as it was. I am here. I am on a bench. My feet are on the ground. I am next to him. We are here. The grass is so soft. That had been my first thought when we'd arrived to tour the house. *The grass is so soft.* I dug my feet down into the ground at the edge of the pond, trying to find that softness again, even among the newly dead blades. Of course, I'd learn that much of what I thought was grass that first day was actually weeds.

But the weeds were soft, too.

It's Called Hope

"I've got to show you my baby," the straight white woman in white jeans says to me. She's been trying to chat up the gays at the piano bar for a while. Now it's my turn. We're in Province-town, just after the Fourth of July. It's a slow week. This year, 2021, they've moved the piano to the outdoor deck instead of inside where we normally congregate. What we lose in close-ness, we gain in public safety. "I've got to show you my baby," the woman says again. She looks to be a little past middle age, whatever that means. She's relaxed and happy; her nails were recently and expensively done. She wants to make friends. Her husband, a sunburnt guy with a fluffy white mustache, has gone to smoke, and she's just made a big deal of kicking him out for his bad habit. She's fun! "I've got to show you my baby"—she's already scrolling through her phone when I realize we're in con-versation. She turns the screen to me when she finds the right photo. She shows me a sleeping black puppy, curled up on an empty queen-size bed. This is the baby.

In the winter, when it seemed likely we'd get vaccinations, David and I had cautiously booked a trip to Provincetown, an artists colony on the tip of Cape Cod, at the edge of America. It's one of our favorite places to be, because it's not too hot for him and not too cold for me, it's surrounded by water, there's art and performance and food. And it's a place that has, for decades, been a destination and a refuge for LGBTQ people. Provincetown is the only place I hold his hand in public and feel safe. And because of that, it's holy to me.

We'd booked the trip and hoped and waited. One of David's mentors taught him to always know when his next vacation was. He would even ask it of David randomly: "When's your next vacation?" It was a reminder that rest and rejuvenation are a part of the work. The pause makes the work possible. After Rick died in May, we asked each other if we should still go, as we'd just been gone for two weeks and our lives had been turned upside down, and we'd be traveling back up the coast to Maine for his Viking funeral in August. But we decided that some distance would help us see the chaotic present, and ourselves in it, in scale.

David went up before me. I'd stayed behind in Baltimore for my father's surprise retirement party. There was a moment I wasn't sure I could make both the party and our travel plans work. But after what I'd learned from Rick and from the experience I'd had with David closing the chapter of his life, I was renewed in my commitment to show up for what mattered.

Both of my brothers were at the party, and although we hadn't conferred beforehand, all three of us showed up wearing pale-pink dress shirts and blue blazers, like backup singers in a Brooks Brothers–themed doo-wop group. We're very different people, but apparently when our mother tells us, "Look nice," we all reach for the same hanger.

We stood in one of the markets my father had managed for over two decades and listened to co-workers share their love and appreciation for a man who had been not only a co-worker and boss but a mentor, a friend, a supporter, a cheerleader, and a visionary. This was the man that I knew—that we knew—but painted in vibrant shades that I'd never seen. I knew that his tirelessness, and my mother's, had made everything in my life possible. But we never really know who our loved ones are away from us.

When I arrived in Provincetown, I started talking before I even got off the ferry. One of the things I've learned from working at home is that when I go for long periods of time without talking to anyone, I tend to bombard David with a rambling series of stories, thoughts, asides, gossip, and questions the minute he walks in the door. Actually, I do this even when I haven't been cooped up in the house all day. I'm a lot without reason or provocation. I spotted David on the pier and I just launched into it as usual. My father's retirement, my storytelling gig in Philly the day before, my suspicion that something had bitten me at the hotel where I stayed in Boston, how I was glad I don't leave my suitcase or clothes on any soft surface in a hotel for this very reason, my assertion that it's not paranoia if it turns out to be true just one time, the ferry ride, the waves, the two coffees I had this morning! All of which was to say, "The world is so strange and so wild and sometimes so beautiful and I am so many different versions of myself away from you, but I am trying to share as much of it as I can."

We walked up to our bed-and-breakfast, David carrying my bag so that I could gesticulate wildly with both hands. Along the way we passed the Woodman/Shimko Gallery, an art dealer I'd visited before; I had always wistfully wished I could take some of the work on the walls home. We'd never been able to buy a painting, though. We hadn't even talked about it. Displayed on the gallery's porch was a tall painting of a huge silver-white cloud against a black sky. It took my breath away for a second and I paused, then I picked back up where I'd left off on my monologue.

In our room, I washed my face, still talking, changed my clothes, and finally stopped for just a second. David seized the opportunity.

"I was walking around earlier," he said, "and I found a painting I think we should buy."

And I knew. Before he took me down and showed it to me, I knew it was the same painting that had taken my breath away.

There are bumper stickers all over Provincetown that implore you to "Eat at Sal's," and I'm incredibly suggestible, so I got David and me reservations at Sal's Place. It's a tight, cozy, frequently very warm Italian restaurant in a house on the east end of Commercial Street. The bumper stickers are a bit of guerrilla marketing that stemmed, I'd been told, from an ongoing legal dispute between the owner of Sal's and her next-door neighbor. I don't know who is right or wrong here—blessings to all involved—but I'm delighted by using swag to escalate an acrimonious relationship. If you're going through an ugly divorce, make souvenir mugs.

Sal's Place had received special permission during the pandemic to add additional seating on the beach below the restaurant. When we arrived at five—the only slot I could get—we were led down to the waterline, where they'd set up rows of simple wooden tables, each with two wooden chairs behind them, side by side. It felt like we'd stumbled upon the set of a play, the tables all facing the audience of the horizon, waiting. I was struck by the simplicity. It was austere and yet so elegant.

A barefoot server came and took our order as the other tables slowly started filling up. Other couples, a cadre of friends, a multigenerational family with two young children who ran down to the water and played in the waves. One of the kids wandered out a little far and, moving as one, all the adults on the beach lifted their heads and watched to make sure she was safe.

There's a thing that happens when you're in a group, in an audience, all watching the same thing. Without our intervention, our heartbeats sync up, our breaths start to align. Our bodies become a community, the pieces moving in concert. I wondered if that's what was happening on that beach. I wondered if anyone was feeling, as I was in that moment, in awe at this tender place that was made for us, this small heaven.

Before we got married, David told me about a practice that one of his mentors used in his marriage. Every year, David said, the mentor and his spouse would have a state-of-the-union conversation. They'd rehash what was working and what wasn't, to find the places where they were out of sync. Most important, they would ask each other, "Do you still want to do this?" The question scared the bejesus out of me, because what if someone is like, "Actually, no. Thanks!" What then?

It felt like a lot of pressure, at least in concept. Like a progress report. Sitting across from each other in business suits and Windsor-knotted neckties, each of us holding a ream of papers with scatterplot graphs and spreadsheets. We each take a sip of coffee, lean back, and say simultaneously, "Well, let's get into it, shall we?"

What David's mentor was talking about was the kind of open, vulnerable questioning that can shore up a marriage;

what I was thinking of was the Pepsi board-of-directors meeting from *Mommie Dearest*. I mulled both options. It was scarier, wasn't it, to look each other in the face and leave room for doubt? Better to just treat marriage like a long car ride when you're a kid, barely paying attention in the back seat, looking out the window, entertaining yourself, and occasionally asking, "Are we there yet?"

The state-of-the-union conversation was a structured way of looking at what we were moving away from and questioning what we were moving toward. It was information. Information didn't have to be dangerous. The ream of papers we held could just be old-school printed MapQuest directions, and the question we'd ask could be, "Should we take another route?" But we were at the beginning then and I didn't know that.

We talked about when to have this conversation and we settled on our first anniversary, which, in retrospect, was probably not the best idea. Imagine having a performance evaluation at your job during your office birthday party. Sitting in front of your break room cake, confronted with anonymized peer feedback and a lower-than-expected raise. We were in Wisconsin on our anniversary, at the wedding of two friends. David had married them, and I'd been asked to lead a storytelling hour about the couple at the reception. He and I were shaping up to be a lovely double act, but please, no reviews. We stayed the weekend at a gorgeous bed-and-breakfast and had our anniversary dinner in a quiet corner of a small nearby restaurant. And somewhere between the appetizer and the entrée, we both pulled out a metaphorical ream of paper and took a deep breath.

Neither one of us had any major complaints or concerns, but the way we'd set the conversation up invited nitpicking and critique. We had precious little data on our marriage to go off at that point, and so we reached clumsily for anything to help fill the space. What it should have been was each of us saying, "Do you still want to do this?" and the other answering, "Duh," and then us having steak and talking about what really mattered: whether we thought the character Renee on *The Americans* was a spy. Instead, the conversation devolved into tiny domestic discomforts, probably about dishes or spending money or something—neither one of us remembers anymore; that's how much time and experience grind down what seemed nearly insurmountable in the beginning.

The next year, we went to dinner at a restaurant high above Baltimore. We sat by the window and ignored the view as we had another unhappy, awkward state-of-the-union conversation. We shared dessert silently and went home, deflated.

The third year, we were both out of town separately for work. It still hadn't occurred to us to have the conversation on any other day, so we just didn't have it at all.

The fourth year, we sat in the house we'd recently purchased, where the garden was trying to take us down and the neighbors across the street might be, too, and decided we were done having the conversation. We asked each other, "Do you still want to do this?" but "this" was "hurting our own feelings conducting an evaluation of our marriage," and we answered, "Actually, no. Thanks!"

I don't think there's anything wrong with the method; I just think we were both too new and nervous to get it right. "Do you still want to do this?" isn't a question for the beginning of the journey. The question is a cairn, like the one we'd left at the top of Black Butte, something for the middle of the trek. It scared me then because I didn't know how you get up the mountain. I didn't know that the answer is simply, "You just do. And it helps if you have no idea what it'll take."

What we've found is that the conversation isn't an evaluation or a summary of this thing we're making so much as a way of asking the other, "Who are you now? Who are we now? How do we move on to whatever comes next together?"

My father told me he had great plans for retirement. He served on boards and at his and my mother's church; he would have time to volunteer even more. He wanted to start a nonprofit benefiting the community. He keeps busy. He cares about the work. He was excited, he said, but also it was daunting. No one tells you how to live the next part. How to get started. It's up to you; the future rolls out endlessly, but how to step into it?

I'd never thought about that. I think I assume that everyone knows what they're doing except for me and many politicians. But it occurred to me that an experience of life is that you keep encountering new versions of it, with less and less external instruction about what to do. I think this is why the jump from high school to college can be so challenging at times. It was for me. I leapt in with both feet and quickly got overwhelmed. Coming back home after that initial jump had been crushing. I felt for years, through bad jobs and misadventures, that I'd squandered all the potential that had launched me from Baltimore. I know now that's not true. But I'd only recently learned that I didn't need to keep telling myself a story of endings. This life, too, is one of constant beginnings.

I wondered what it must feel like to be him, sitting on a stool in the front of his party, listening to tributes. I wondered if any of us ever really understands how much we mean to the world while we're in it.

———

On our last day in Provincetown, David and I returned to the gallery to finalize our purchase of the painting, by the artist Adam Thomas, and arrange for shipping. Any fear that our enthusiasm for it had simply been a byproduct of our excitement to be on the Cape was wiped away the minute we encountered it again. It is ostensibly a painting of a black sky full of ominous clouds, but the first impression is just cloud. One tall, billowing tower of a cloud. There's a halo of white light glowing at the top edge, as if the moon is just beyond the bounds of the canvas, but there's no way of really telling where we are. In the center there's a huge, puffy thunderhead above a cascade of looser clouds that continue all the way down to the bottom of the painting, where they dissolve into a gray-black gradient. One of the gallerists suggested that we display the painting with a light above it, which would bring out the thin ridge of the horizon at the bottom. I looked closer; I hadn't seen it before. But, there at the very bottom, no more than a centimeter high, is a strip of fiery dark orange. Sunrise or sunset. I didn't know which. We filled out the shipping information and, on the form, I was surprised to find the painting's name. It hadn't occurred to me to ask what it was called. But this piece of art—mysterious and foreboding, overwhelming, dazzling; beguiling, and inscrutable, and beyond our means; waiting there for us—its name is *Hope*.

"I've got to show you my baby," the woman at the piano bar says. She's having a wonderful time. Life is good, like her husband's shirt says. She's on vacation. She likes her hubby, even though he smokes. She loves her baby, the little black puppy. What a life they've made after all this time. The night air is invigorating, and the music—covers played on a piano and sung by Todd Alsup—is bringing back happy memories.

Her husband returns, loping through the courtyard. He takes a seat next to her and they fall into conversation. I slide closer to David. I am here now. And David is here now. And it's easy in this moment.

After a while, David and I decide to keep moving. We pay our tab and step off the porch, heading across the courtyard of the restaurant. Just then, the singer starts in on "Your Song," and some part of me that I don't think I knew about lights up. I love this song, I discover. I understand this song. Is this an understanding that I've always had? I don't know. We turn back and I hang off the railing like a baby angel in a Renaissance painting as the singer croons, *How wonderful life is while you're in the world.*

After it's over, David takes my hand in his and we walk out of the courtyard and into the street. We pass the gallery, where the easel that had held *Hope* now stands empty. And we keep moving, walking through the darkness, the road ahead like an ocean, a constellation, a garden, a borderless house, a life, an apocalypse, a thunderhead over a sliver of sunlight, a day—not the best day, but a good one. This is not the beginning. And this is not the end.

So we stay that way, hand in hand, under the stars, walking for a good long while.

Acknowledgments

I discovered with my first book that people who read the acknowledgments are a special club. It's like having the password to party at a speakeasy, which is hilarious because the acknowledgments are not a hidden event. They are literally sitting here at the end. All you have to do is turn the page, Grover. But only the cool kids do. *So, welcome to the after-party!*

First of all, I think we should acknowledge Patti LaBelle, don't you? Patti, I am sorry my story about meeting you did not make it into this book. You join my other beloved icons who I care about very deeply but have not written about in a book: my twin Chris Newcomer and my life coach Jarrod Markman. As this book arcs toward hope through the darkness of the pando years, it is arcing toward you and our friendship. Everyone, please come see the show that Chris and I are always saying we're going to write called *Two Miss Piggies*. Tickets are going fast!

I continue to be lucky and blessed to work with the most phenomenal people in publishing. Thank you, Sara Weiss, for your wisdom, your patience, your brilliance, and your compassion. Thank you to Sydney Collins for your brilliance, as well, your organization, your hard work, and your wisdom. EMILY ISAYEFF! TAYLOR NOEL! Literally a dream team, you make everything possible, you're endlessly positive, I just love you so much. Rachel Ake designed the cover for this book and *Here for It* and is actually a genius. Everybody loves these covers! I love these covers! People pick up these books because of these covers! Your artwork makes such a huge difference and I appreciate it.

Thanks to the whole team at Ballantine Books, including Jennifer Hershey, Kara Welsh, Kim Hovey, Meghan Whalen, and Kelly Chian. I am so grateful to work with you.

Thanks to my indefatigable agent, Anna Sproul-Latimer, and the whole team at Neon Literary. You're incredible! Thanks also to my team at A3—Amy, Antoni, Martin, and Ron—and Alex at Anonymous Content.

Steven Gross is a brilliant and wise soul and a wonderful friend. I am grateful to know you and so grateful for the smart, thoughtful, crucial editorial work you put into this book. I want to keep working together forever!

To a person named Joseph who was wearing a fuzzy leopard-print hat in ninety-degree weather and stopped me on the street in 2022 to excitedly talk about the babysitting chapter in *Here for It,* that was truly one of the most incredible experiences of my life. It made my night, my week, my summer. We have never seen each other again. I do not think I dreamt this. What a wild thing!

To the person who stopped me on the street the next morning and said, "Hey! I'm reading your book right now." And then paused for a very long time before saying, "It's not bad." Thank you, too!

So many people have been extremely kind and generous about all my books and all of my works, and I am deeply grateful. Thanks for stopping me or emailing me (I AM SORRY IF I HAVEN'T RESPONDED; AS YOU HAVE JUST READ, I'M HAVING A MIDLIFE CRISIS) or DM'ing me or just reading the book and telling a friend about it. Thanks to that audiobook-listening squad! I loved talking to you!

I've had the pleasure of visiting so many Zoom book clubs

over the last few years, and each one has been a delight and an honor. Invite me to your Zoom book club! I promise to only be a little weird! (Best way to do this is to email me directly, btw.)

WHERE WOULD I BE WITHOUT LIBRARIANS AND LIBRARY SUPPORT STAFF? NOWHERE. NONEXISTENT. FILE NOT FOUND! Oh, librarians, I just love you so much and I'm so grateful for you and the hugely important work that you do. I know that so many of you have faced years of political and sometimes personal attacks for doing your jobs, for spreading knowledge (the most dangerous thing), and for keeping the doors open and the services free or low-priced. But what you do is vital to our nation, and it does not go unnoticed. Thank you for opening a universe of possibility for me, and thank you for supporting books like mine, even when it's hard. Thank you in particular but not exclusively to those at the Enoch Pratt Free Library, Free Library of Philadelphia, Baltimore County Public Library, Carroll County Public Library, Skokie Public Library, Ashland Public Library, Anne Arundel Public Library, Hartford Public Library, Prince Georges County Memorial Library, and Howard County Library.

Thank you to Jenna Bush Hager and the staff at *Today* for championing me and my book; it changed my life. Thank you also to Ann Patchett, Lin-Manuel Miranda, Phoebe Robinson, Cree Summer, Judith Light, Peter Spears, Alena Smith, Pamela Adlon, Isabel Kallman, Laura Mayes, Jill Daniel, Tara Schuster, Sarah Ruhl, Lynn Nottage, and the folks at *ELLE* magazine for giving influential shout-outs and in so many other ways supporting my work.

Thanks, for the same reason, to President Barack Obama. (Just kidding, he has NOT put me on his end-of-year list but—you know what—life is long! It's never too late to do the right thing!)

Despite being a menace, I have been able to make writer-friends and friend-friends who help me be better on and off the page. Thanks in particular to Aman Goyal, Caleb Johnson, Philip Ellis, John Fram, Tre Johnson, Nicole Chung, AZ Espinosa, L Feldman, Kyle Toth, Kristen Norine, Bella Desai, Ken Greller, Chasten Buttigieg, Sean Simon, Jackie Goldfinger, Becky Wright, Bren Thomas, and Rebecca Adelsheim.

I've also received such kindness and support from a great many Bookstagram accounts, including ShelfbyShelf, BookishandBlack, TheStacksPod, JanaiReadsBooks, MattyandtheBooks, HeyBookZaddy, ReadwithMason, WellReadBlackGirl, BowtiesandBooks, OhYouRead, AudioShelMe, BooksnBlazers, Nikis.bookish.diary, LiteraryPengwyns, and BooksNatureMagic.

If you are supporting me on TikTok, thank you also! I do not know how to use it very well, but I feel your energy from over here!

Booksellers, particularly independent booksellers, are the beating heart of our industry and have made it possible for me to continue writing books. Thank you for hand-selling copies, welcoming me for events, writing shelf reviews, and all the myriad things you do to make the world better. Thanks in particular but certainly not exclusively to Rosamond at Broadside Bookshop, Julia and so many more at Greedy Reads, Debbie at A Likely Story, Kathleen at Andersons Bookshop, Sissy and the whole team at Parnassus, Daven and Joe at Charm City Books, Emma and everyone at Books Are Magic, Laurie, Emily, and so many more at East City Bookshop, Hannah, Diana, and Malik at Loyalty Books, plus the folks at Solid State Books, Politics and Prose, Uncle Bobbie's, East End Bookshop, and so many more.

My therapist, Brian. The years we worked together were so

hard and it was so hard to find hope. But through our work, hope appeared. I appreciate you; I thank you.

Thank you to my wonderful mother-in-law, Rachel, for your support, your kindness, and your love. Thanks to my Aunt Pat and my Aunt Barbara for always letting me know how proud you are of me. Thanks to my Uncle Mike for showing me life-long support and love. Thanks for being a good friend to my dad, too. That means a lot.

My family: Stephen and Kathleen and Jeffrey and Karen, I am grateful for your love and your support and I love you and your kids!

My parents, Bob and Judi, have spent over forty years finding new ways of showing me that I am valuable in this world, I am wanted, and that the things I make don't define me but that they matter. I love you and I'm grateful for you.

David. My love. "This is the sound of voices two, helping each other to make it through."

Well, anyway, as with every party when I'm ready for people to go, I'm going to start subtly yawning and bustling about in the kitchen. No, no! Don't get up. This was fun! We should do it again sometime. But what's a party without favors? *If you'd like to see special photos from some of the essays in this book, visit:* rericthomas.com/afterparty.

Thanks to *you* for coming to my acknowledgments party. They sometimes feel a bit what I imagine a retirement party might feel like: getting to see and say thank you to the people who make it possible for you to do the work you do. Frankly, we should all be able to get the affirmation of a retirement party whenever we want it.

Or maybe not retirement, because I presume you'll still want to get paid. What about lifetime achievement? Who can say what all can be achieved in a lifetime? Maybe we should lower the bar. I feel like people should be able to declare lifetime-achievement-award status at any moment. Like the election pundits who are like, "I've seen enough! I'm calling it!" That, but for your contribution to humanity. The award should also be called "I've Seen Enough."

If you're giving the award to Jennifer Lopez, the award should be called "I've Seen *Enough*."

But, in general, the award should be for living, not achieving, I think. That's the miracle.

About the Author

R. ERIC THOMAS is the bestselling author of *Here for It: Or, How to Save Your Soul in America,* a Lambda Literary Award finalist, and the YA novel *Kings of B'more,* a Stonewall Honor book. Both books were also featured as Read with Jenna book club picks on *Today.* He is a television writer (Apple TV+'s *Dickinson,* FX's *Better Things*), a Lambda Literary Award–winning playwright, and the long-running host of The Moth in Philadelphia. For four years, he was a senior staff writer at *ELLE* online, where he wrote the popular "Eric Reads the News" column.

rericthomas.com
Facebook.com/R.Eric.Thomas
Instagram, Twitter: @oureric